THE WOMAN AND THE WAY

The Woman and the Way

A Marian Path to Jesus

George T. Montague, S.M.

Servant Publications
Ann Arbor, Michigan

Except where the abbreviation NAB is cited, all Scripture
texts are translations by the author. Where NAB is cited,
the Scripture texts are taken from the *New American Bible
with Revised New Testament,* copyright © 1986
Confraternity of Christian Doctrine, Washington, D.C.,
and are used by permission.

Published by Servant Publications
P.O. Box 8617
Ann Arbor, Michigan 48107

Cover design by Gerald L. Gawronski/The Look
Cover art, Leonardo DaVinci *The Madonna of
the Rocks*/Erich Lessing/Art Resource

94 95 96 97 98 10 9 8 7 6 5 4 3 2

Printed in the United States of America

Library of Congress Cataloging-in-Publication Data

Montague, George T., S.M.
    The woman and the way : a marian path to Jesus / George
T. Montague.
        p. cm.
    "Charis books."
    Includes bibliographical references.
    ISBN 0-89283-856-6
    1. Spiritual formation—Catholic Church. 2. Mary, Blessed
Virgin, Saint—Theology. 3. Catholic Church—Adult educa-
tion. I. Title.
BX2350.7.M66 1994
248.4'82—dc20   93-48824

Contents

Introduction

I wanted more of God.

I knew God wanted more of me.

But I couldn't give him more because there were parts of me that should have been mine but weren't. They were out of my control. I couldn't give God the more I wanted to give. I couldn't give God the more he wanted of me.

But I learned. I learned by giving myself to Jesus' mother and letting her lead me. With her I began to see the areas of my life that didn't look like those of her firstborn Son—my speech, my memory, my thoughts and fantasies, my heart. And although I am still a long way from living my total consecration to Jesus and Mary, I've learned a measure of self-possession that makes living that consecration more of a daily reality. I've also learned that my wayward tendencies have roots that only God can heal. And I trust the process. I trust the journey. I trust him. I trust her.

THAT, IN BRIEF, is what this book is about. If your experience is anything like mine, I hope this book will help you.

The Bible speaks of God's plan for us as a *way*. The Wisdom books give a lot of practical directions about that way. But they do more. They image Wisdom as a woman who invites us to her banquet and instructs us in the ways of God (Prv 8:1-9:11). She is a bride, she is also a mother: "Mother-like she will meet him, /like a young bride she will embrace him, /nourish him with the bread of understanding /and give him the water of learning to drink" (Sir 15:2-3, NAB). Solomon becomes lyrical in praising Lady Wisdom, and he prays that she be given him as his life's companion (Wis 7:7-11:1).

God's wisdom became flesh in Jesus born of Mary (1 Cor 1:24). Jesus is the *way* (Jn 14:6). As the epiphany of God's wisdom, however, he is also companioned by his mother. She models the response to Jesus. She walks with us on the way. She believes that all the Lord promised will come true. Like Lady Wisdom who invites us to her banquet, she instructs us, as she did the servants at the Messianic banquet of Cana, "Do whatever he tells you."

Mary is Lady Wisdom. She is also the mother, Jesus' mother but ours as well because Jesus gave her to us from the cross. From her we can learn the way of Wisdom. Such is the meaning of *The Woman and the Way.*

In this book I share only what I have received. It is a cord braided of three strands, each of them gifts.

The first is Scripture: my inspiration and the stuff of my teaching for nearly four decades. I call on the riches of the Word here not in a highly technical sense but rather from the standpoint of its spiritual nourishment.

The second strand is my own spiritual journey, coupled with my experience of companioning others as they travel their own way. Alongside the mountains and valleys of my own road, I was called to spend some twenty years in the work of religious formation, including six years as a seminary rector and another six as a director of novices in Nepal and India. Through many years as a spiritual director for laity, priests, religious, and college students, I have received more than I have given.

A third strand is the particular Marianist spirituality in which I was formed, especially the work of Venerable William

Joseph Chaminade, who formed groups of lay people and founded two religious communities in the early nineteenth century. This priest wrote and spoke much about how the Holy Spirit uses Mary to form us into the likeness of Jesus Christ. Being a practical spiritual guide, he also commended to his disciples a "system of virtues" as a way of cooperating with the action of the Holy Spirit and Mary. He was heir to a great stream of spirituality known as "the French school," which inspired many other religious founders of the seventeenth, eighteenth, and nineteenth centuries.

I have included this strand because my experience has convinced me that Fr. Chaminade's program is an eminently practical way to grow in holiness, and it corresponds to a widespread thirst today for such growth through Mary.

This book basically follows the outline of Fr. Chaminade's program, but expands his development with insights from my study and prayer with the Scriptures, baptismal spirituality, the silence of the memories (an expansion of Chaminade's interior silences), and bodily awareness. This last dimension can be considered an expansion of Chaminade's concern for bringing even bodily communication (as distinct from words) under the influence of the Holy Spirit. I owe my growth in this area of spirituality particularly to my six-year experience in India and Nepal, where I learned much about the integration of body and spirit in prayer.

Along with these three strands, there is one characteristic of all Christian spirituality to which the program of growth in this book gives special attention. We do not grow as isolated individuals. We grow as members of a community, for Jesus calls us to be part of his body. This community is first of all the church, but for most of us it finds expression in a smaller unit of that church: our parish or a small group within it, a religious or lay community, a prayer group or a Bible study, or the most basic unit of society and the church, our family. Many of us belong to several kinds of communities at once. If we are to be a light to the world, a city set on a mountaintop, then a great deal of our growth is going to be in our relations with one another. This book supposes and even emphasizes that dimension of discipleship in community.

HOW TO USE THIS BOOK

Readers may choose to use this book in different ways. It can provide nourishment and challenge merely in private reading. Or it may be used under the guidance of one's spiritual director. Given the importance of the community dimension in discipleship, one of the most fruitful ways would be to use the text as the basis for a faith sharing group.

Unlike a discussion group which exchanges ideas, a faith sharing group uses an experiential process whereby the participants share their attempts to live the truths or the virtues under discussion. They focus not on "what should this be saying to us or the world in general?" but on "what is this saying to *me today*?" They talk about their personal experience rather than the experience of others, being careful not to moralize, homilize, or give advice.

Furthermore, the individuals in a faith sharing group speak of *recent* experience—preferably their attempts within the last week or two to embody this truth or live this virtue in their lives. I have gleaned much from the insights shared in such groups. After this introduction, you will find guidelines and a recommended format for using this book with a faith sharing group.

If you are using this book as an individual, you may choose to move through it at your own pace. It is not meant to be read all at once. Rather it should be read, prayed over, and put into practice in sections, as you use the meditations, exercises, questions, and prayers to focus on one virtue at a time.

In group use, the group can decide on its own pace. Some

chapters may be so fruitful that groups may wish to spend more than one meeting on them. A group may decide to break the sharing of the book down into eight- or nine-week units (as is often done in Bible studies in parishes). For example, a fall unit might be done before Christmas and a winter and spring unit around the time of Lent. Another spring and summer unit could be planned for the Easter season. Such an approach presupposes that groups would typically study a chapter each week and meet for eight or nine weeks during each unit, since there are twenty-four chapters in all.

The meditations are for personal use, as are most of the exercises. These meditations and exercises appear at the end of many sections in the chapters. When the group meets, individuals may wish to share their experience of the meditations or the exercises, or which question in the "Steps on the Journey" at the end of the chapter struck home to them. In group sharing, each individual should be free to use whatever approach he or she wishes in reporting about personal experience with the virtue. If the group wishes, it can use one or all of the questions in "Steps on the Journey" to initiate sharing, but these should be helps to personal sharing and not rigidly adhered to. The closing prayer at the end of each chapter could well be used as the concluding prayer, either of one's personal meditation or of the group sharing.

One of the strongest benefits of this spirituality of the virtues is its enduring value in personal and group application. Once you have been through the book, you may find it fruitful to go through it again, either right away or at a later stage in your life, since this program is not geared to any specific chronological age and assumes a lifelong growth in the virtues. There are new challenges at each new stage of our lives, and this program can be of help wherever you may be in your journey.

In any case, this book presupposes prayer. It assumes that you will approach a particular virtue not as a mere academic study but meditatively, using Scripture for your personal prayer. This book is also oriented toward practical action. Action ought to be a response to grace, or better perhaps, grace in action.

When Jesus came to the end of his Sermon on the Mount, he spoke about two kinds of people. The one kind built their house on sand, the other on rock. The one who builds on sand hears the words of Jesus but doesn't put them into practice. The one who builds on rock hears the words and *does* them. In fact, if you are engaged in some form of ministry, it will be a good laboratory for learning these virtues. Serving others often heals our own brokenness (Is 58:6-11).

If you don't want your life to be changed, put this book down right now. People don't read recipe books for entertainment; they're looking for directions on how to cook. This book supplies a recipe for living the Christian life. This is the reason for the meditations, the practical exercises, and the questions for self-examination. This book will change your life if you follow the directions!

I encourage you to keep a spiritual journal of your reflections, your experiences, and what the Lord is teaching you. Besides helping you remember your journey at a later date, this regular practice will help you discern patterns of God's grace and calling in your life, and patterns of your own struggles. You may want to share some of this information with your spiritual director, a trusted friend, your spouse, or your faith sharing group.

The topics follow in an orderly progression. First, the foundation in Part One: the Christian life boils down to a relationship with a person, Jesus Christ. Relating to him in faith implies receiving the gifts he has to give, including two gifts he explicitly points to in the Gospels: the Holy Spirit and Mary, spouse of the Spirit, mother of Jesus, and our mother.

Part Two entitled "Taking Hold" concerns our preliminary efforts to take responsibility for our lives. Various practical sectors are offered as "laboratories" for doing this—the discipline of our body, our speech, our memory, mind and imagination, the freedom from the tyranny of moods, and availability to others. Our primary aim in this part of the journey is not *control* so much as *awareness* of our tendencies.

Part Three, "Letting Go," probes deeper into the roots of our negative tendencies. Why do we act or re-act the way we do? Why is the effort at control and discipline so difficult? What healing do we need at a deeper level? Here we look at the obstacles to growth: the outer ones like opposition, seductions, trials, and temptations, but especially the inner ones like our weaknesses, hesitations, and fears. We learn that the only way to ultimate victory at this deeper level is a greater trust in God, allowing him more and more to take control of our lives.

Part Four, "Letting God," concerns the final stage of letting the Lord shine through our lives. It is the summit to which we ultimately aspire. We do not cling even to the great spiritual gifts God has given us but look to God himself as our sole security. We become less self-conscious even of the good we do, becoming transparent like Mary, who wanted nothing more than to magnify the Lord and be available for his purposes.

While the virtues in this system build upon one another, they do not correspond exactly to what ascetical-mystical theology has called the purgative, illuminative, and unitive stages. These rather discrete phases of the spiritual life include definite signs of passage from one to the other. Ordinarily one does not return to the work of the earlier stage.

The sequence described in this book is more like a spiral. We move from one virtue to the other until we reach the last. Then we return to the beginning and start over, enlightened by the experience and wisdom gained from the cycle we have just completed. In following this sequence we will always find ourselves at a deeper level of understanding and growth.

I wish to thank in a special way those who have helped in the preparation of this book. Sr. Marcy Loehrlein, F.M.I., was very helpful by her critical reading and suggestions concerning earlier versions of the manuscript. Mrs. Melba Fisher gets much of the credit for formulating the questions for reflection and sharing. Further, some faith sharing groups among faculty, staff, and students on the campus of St. Mary's University in San Antonio, Texas, provided a good testing ground for this presentation. Their responses often contributed insights I had never considered before. For all of these I am deeply grateful.

George T. Montague, S.M.
November 15, 1993

Guidelines and Format for Faith Sharing Groups

GUIDELINES

1. Focus on a *sharing of faith* rather than on a *discussion*. Each person in the group should come prepared to share on the particular virtue being studied: *How have I tried to live this virtue since our last meeting?*

2. In *response* to sharing, others should refrain from commenting (unless briefly affirming), preaching, or giving advice. The sharing should not get off into discussion. Any "experts" present should be equal participants and not assume a dominant or teaching role. Occasional periods of silence can be viewed as beneficial, so that everyone feels comfortable in either sharing or in being momentarily silent. The leader makes prudent judgments as needed.

3. The ideal *group size* is eight to ten persons, a size which should allow each person to have sufficient time to share.

4. The group decides *how often and how long* they wish to meet. An agreed-upon coordinator can serve as the group's contact person. Weekly or biweekly meetings have proven to be the most successful.

5. Since this is primarily a sharing group, *rotation of leadership* among the members seems to work best. The leader for the

day opens with prayer, welcomes everyone, keeps the sharings faithful to the meeting's purpose, discourages persons from dominating or being too lengthy, keeps the group within the time frame, and brings the meeting to closure with prayer. After someone briefly explains the assigned material, a leader is selected for the next meeting.

6. *Trust and confidentiality* are essential to the group's effectiveness and growth. It is essential that everyone in the group feel that their sharing is respected and that no one in the group will sit in judgment. Nor will anything shared in confidence be conveyed outside the group.

7. *Everyone* in the group takes *responsibility* for assisting the group to be faithful to its goals.

FORMAT

- Two minutes: Opening prayer by designated leader.

- Thirty to forty-five minutes: Leader begins by sharing experiences and insights from praying about and practicing the virtue which is the object of this week's focus. Others in the group are invited and encouraged to do the same. How have those present lived the virtues since the last meeting— in family, parish, community, school, study, and work environments? The questions provided in this book may be used as starters, but the most important benefit is to share personal experiences.

- Two minutes: Someone gives a brief explanation of the next topic (the virtue which will be the focus until the group meets again).

- One minute: Someone volunteers to lead the next meeting. Information is shared with the group as needed.

- Two minutes: Designated leader brings group to closure with prayer.

Part One

❀

Jesus and His Gifts

Jesus and His Gifts

The journey of discipleship is not a program for self-improvement or self-help. There are plenty of books around that tell you how to lose weight, or how to become more productive or more popular. Discipleship is our response to a personal initiative on God's part. Before we decide to do anything even for God, God comes to meet us in his Son. Jesus offers us his life, his suffering, his death, his resurrection, his Word, his Holy Spirit—and his mother. All is gift. All is response to gift. All we need to do is say, "Yes!"

Before exploring the stages of growth in this gift-response relationship, it is important to look at the Giver and his gifts. For here we find the wellspring of energy that impels us throughout the journey. But we will first look at some of the ways our rich tradition has imaged spiritual growth.

ONE

Images of Spiritual Growth

THE SPIRITUAL MASTERS have tried to capture the mystery of Christian growth under various images. St. John of the Cross spoke of a journey through the darkness of night to the light of day, or the climbing of a mountain, the ascent of Mount Carmel. St. John Climacus spoke of a spiritual ladder. St. Teresa compared it to moving from one spiritual mansion to another. The Little Flower focused on growth in spiritual childhood. The Fathers of the Eastern Church spoke of deification or glorification. St. Ignatius of Loyola and many other spiritual masters advocated the imitation of Jesus. St. Benedict taught continuing conversion.[1]

From a secular perspective, many modern social scientists have delved into the stages of personal psychological growth. The names of Levinson, Kohlberg, Selman, Erikson, Piaget, and Fowler immediately come to mind, each of whom concentrated on different dimensions of human development. Efforts have even been made to correlate these various psychological stages with one another and with the spiritual theology of St. John of the Cross.[2]

The so-called French school of spirituality, from which Fr. Chaminade and many others drew much of their inspiration, stressed *conformity* with Christ. They understood conformity to mean not merely imitating Jesus but union with him in his mysteries, which would encompass the various facets of his being and his life such as the incarnation, infancy, public life, cross, and resurrection.

By entering into these mysteries, we seek to share the dispositions of Jesus—his attitudes, his convictions, his holy passions. And what is the best way to enter into those dispositions? To look upon Jesus with the intuitive eyes of his mother, Mary. For Fr. Chaminade, the privileged act of devotion to Mary means union with Mary in prayer—or looking at Jesus through her eyes.

To grow under Mary's influence also means to grow as community, for as mother she symbolizes the heart of God's family. By concluding the Constitution on the Church with a chapter on Our Lady, the Second Vatican Council emphasized Mary's being a role model of the church as community. Any program of growth, any progress in the virtues, must have a corporate dimension. God doesn't call us to be lone rangers or spiritual mountaineers, even in Christian service. We are called to be a people united in a common mission.

Do we need this kind of spirituality today? How many parishes boast of a brilliant minister who can't work with the parish's other gifted ministers? What is missing? A spirituality and a formative process for *growing together in Christ*. We need strong individuals, yes, but even more we need people who can work with others, people who are capable of team work, of listening and interacting. We need leaders who can empower others, who can spot the gifts of the persons in their group, affirm them, and call them forth for a common mission.

BIBLICAL IMAGES

Nearly all of the developmental images mentioned thus far are drawn in some way from the Bible. But Scripture doesn't necessarily use those images for the individual spiritual growth addressed by these later authors. As a unique book with its own message, its own approach, and its own interests, we need to allow the Bible to speak to us on its own terms.

To be truthful, the authors of the Old Testament didn't express much concern for an individual's progress in the interior life. Biblical spirituality is more tribal or communitarian, primarily concerned with the survival and growth of the community. The crucial information revolves around what's happening in the ongoing history of God's people and in the history of the surrounding world.

If you read two works written at approximately the same period, one nonbiblical and the other biblical, the difference can be striking. For example, the *Bhagavad Gita* and chapters 40 through 55 of Isaiah (called Second Isaiah) were both written about five hundred years before Christ. The first carries an intense focus on individual piety and growth toward enlightenment, with no concern for history and little sense of tragedy.

Second Isaiah, on the other hand, is intensely concerned with history, with a people who have experienced their God through a religious-political saving action which has reversed decades of tragedy. The author focuses on how God transformed their tragic history into a meaningful chapter in a broader sacred history, the journey of a people to the fulfillment of all God has promised them.

The *Gita* undoubtedly surpasses Second Isaiah in its preoccupation with individual piety. I find it interesting to fantasize what a conversation between the two authors would have been like. The scriptural author would probably wonder at the other's lack of concern for history and peoplehood and changing the world for the better. And he would wonder what kind of God could possibly *not* be interested in those things. The *Gita*'s author, in turn, would probably be amazed at the other's lack of interest in the inner journey of the individual.

We do find some models of spiritual growth in the Old Testament. Abraham is basically a wanderer who walks in faith. While waiting for the fulfillment of God's promise, he is tested in his fidelity. The author of Genesis sees Abraham as in some way embodying the experience of the whole people of Israel. St. Paul and the Epistle to the Hebrews exploit the figure of Abraham as a model of faith.

We also find the image of the just person who is like a tree planted beside a running stream, one who is fruitful and able to endure even through the dry season (Ps 1; Jer 17:8). Hosea claims that all Israel's fruitfulness comes from the Lord (Hos 14:9). Proverbs 4:18 tells us that "the path of the just is like shining light, that grows in brilliance till perfect day" (NAB).

In most cases, however, references to fruitfulness and growth pertain more to the temporal blessings with which the Lord rewards the just. The Wisdom books contain counsels for righteous and proper conduct, especially for anyone who served in the king's court. But we find mostly "dos" and "don'ts" rather than programs for growth in virtue. In the Old Testament view, a person was either righteous or a sinner. Precious little shows an awareness of *growth* in righteousness, other than the blessings that would increasingly come to those who were faithful.

As something of an exception to this pattern, the Book of Job challenges the old Deuteronomic view that virtue is always rewarded and sin punished in this life. Through successive tragedies, a just man suffers for no apparent reason. Job questions God over and over, only to face the God who questions Job. After he meets the Lord in the storm of a personal faith experience, Job can live with the mystery of his suffering because "my eye has seen you" (Jb 42:5). He has been transformed. The author of the book's prologue and epilogue, however, returns in some way to the older view by rewarding Job with more temporal benefits than before because he had proven faithful under testing.

Within that biblical theme of fidelity, however, lies another image that comes close to inner growth. It is the theme of *strengthening*. Those who trust in the Lord grow in strength:

"He gives strength to the fainting; for the weak he makes vigor abound. Though young men faint and grow weary, and youths stagger and fall, they that hope in the Lord will renew their strength, they will soar as with eagles' wings; they will run and not grow weary, walk and not grow faint" (Is 40:29-31, NAB).

We could say, then, that the Old Testament focuses on trust, fidelity, and perseverance. The just person may go through a period of testing, as Job did, but the Old Testament has no theory of the stages of spiritual growth. The later prophets, particularly Ezekiel and Second Isaiah, do see a pattern of growth for the whole people when they trace the stages of Israel's religious history. They set the pattern for the kind of spiritual biography which perceives God's hand in the individual's life events. Even so, these authors focus primarily on community and its common journey.

In today's atmosphere of heightened individualism, I find it refreshing and challenging to be called back to our deep Christians roots in communal spirituality. Our origins are tribal. And in the tribal culture the individual is imbedded in a larger entity—the family, the tribe, the people.

I spent six years in South Asia as director of Marianist novices for India. Many of them were tribals. One day we received a letter of application that ran something like this: "My name is Arunjan. My father is a farmer; my mother is a housewife at home. My older brother is in the army; another brother works for the post office; my sister is away at nursing school; my younger brother and sister live at home while they are going to school. *Now that you know all about me,* I hope you will let me enter your order." This man's description is typical of the tribal way of thinking: to introduce one's family is to introduce oneself.

Fr. John Kavanaugh, S.J., described a similar experience when he was trying to teach philosophy to a group of African students. He explained Descartes' famous proof for existence:

"I think, therefore, I am." After some discussion, one of the students said, "We in Africa would rather say, '*We* exist, therefore I am.'" This young man was keenly aware that his very being depended on the existence of the tribe.

Looking at our tribal roots makes us realize the importance of "we" even for our personal spiritual growth. It also highlights the importance of fidelity, perseverance, and simply hanging in there with our people, our church, and our community. The ideal Jew is called the "just," and that means the one who lives in right relationships. And the ideal Jewish community was called the *hasidim*, the people who were loyal and faithful in their love for their God and people.

GROWTH IN THE NEW TESTAMENT

As Christians, of course, we read the Old Testament in the light of Jesus and the new community of God's people. The New Testament authors looked back to their communal history to find numerous models for the Christian life. Crossing the sea in the Exodus symbolizes Christian baptism; the desert wanderings remind us of our journey to the promised land; the rock from which water flowed symbolizes Jesus and the Holy Spirit; the Babylonian captivity symbolizes our need for redemption; and, of course, the whole Old Testament is seen as a waiting and longing for the coming Messiah and the kingdom of God.

In this context, it is Paul more than any other biblical author who develops the notion of spiritual growth. The life of love poured into our hearts by the Holy Spirit (Rom 5:5) abounds and overflows. The church is a body that is built up (Eph 4:12), a temple that grows (Eph 2:21-22).

Heir to the Old Testament, Paul thinks of spiritual growth primarily as a community process, though he obviously thinks that the individual grows too. Life is a race to win the crown, a boxing match where every blow counts (1 Cor 9:24-27). In sum, Paul sees the Christian life as a progressive transformation of Christians by the Holy Spirit into the glorious image of the risen Christ (2 Cor 3:17-18).

When the Gospels use the image of journey, it is used not only to bind together the many traditional stories and sayings of Jesus but also to show a deepening understanding of Jesus in the disciples. They do not see clearly until after Jesus' resurrection and the gift of the Holy Spirit; the journey is a learning experience for them. In later spirituality, the concept of journey will become a dominant image for spiritual growth. To be a disciple means to follow Jesus in one's own personal journey, imitating him and learning from him.

Another image we find in the Gospels is that of the seed that grows. The parable of the sower appears in all three synoptics. If the disciples felt their confidence bolstered in the ultimate success of the Master's message, the parable quickly took on a deeper meaning. Jesus explains that the seed is first of all the Word (Mk 4:14), then immediately says that the seed stands for the different hearers of the Word (Mk 4:15-20). The Word of God is living (Heb 4:12), but it lives not in a book but in people who enflesh it in their lives. The disciples are to become the visible, living Word of God! Jesus even calls them the light of the world (Mt 5:14).

But not everyone responds equally. The seed bears fruit according to the readiness of the soil. Conditions in the hearer can either block or foster the growth of the Word. Barren by itself, the soil needs the seed that carries the code of life within it. But neither will the seed bear fruit without the soil. We begin to see the importance of receptivity and the need to cooperate with the new life by eliminating the obstacles to its growth—foundational principles for the spiritual challenge presented in this book.

JOURNEY INWARD, JOURNEY OUTWARD

Following Jesus or growing into conformity with him involves a twofold journey: the journey inward and the jour-

ney outward. We move inward in silence, peace, inner awareness, prayer, the presence of God, and all those other things
associated with inner growth. We move outward in service and
solidarity with others. Our spiritual life from baptism until the
moment we die intertwines those two movements, just as the
ocean tides flow in and out. One movement calls for and pre-
pares the way for the other.

Although the virtues we examine may seem aimed only at
our personal transformation, a closer look will open up a wider
vista. These same virtues are also shaping us for more effective
interaction with others, and ultimately making us sharper
instruments of the Holy Spirit for the transformation of the
world.

The New Testament presents Mary as a model of faith and
as the mother of Jesus. Later generations meditated on this
dual role and combined it with St. Paul's imagery of the community as the body of Christ growing unto perfect maturity.
They found in Jesus' conception and birth a pattern for our
own spiritual transformation. We too are conceived of the
Holy Spirit in our baptism. And just as the Holy Spirit formed
Jesus in the womb of Mary, so he forms us "in the womb of
her motherly tenderness" until we are totally transformed into
Jesus. We shall explore what this means in detail in a later
chapter.

But our spiritual transformation also makes us missionaries,
called to evangelize and share our experience of the good
news of Jesus, wherever God calls us to be beacons of faith.
The words of Mary to the servants at Cana become a missionary command: "Do whatever he tells you." Mary tells us, her
servants, to obey Jesus in whatever he calls us to do for the
service of the church and the Father's kingdom.

Steps on the Journey

1. What model of spiritual growth appeals to you most and why?

2. Have you given much thought in the past to your growth as a disciple of Jesus?

3. What new insight have you gained from this chapter? How will it help your life?

4. How do you feel about being called to be a missionary within your own environment?

5. Have you thought of Mary as involved in any way in your spiritual growth?

Lord Jesus, I thank you for calling me to be your disciple. And I thank you for reminding me that my journey has only begun. I have much to learn and much to unlearn. Enlighten me with your Holy Spirit as you enlightened Mary, that I may accept your call to holiness and make the sacrifices you ask of me to complete my personal journey. Amen.

*The Call
and the Decision*

W E NEED TO UNDERTAKE this spiritual journey from the
very beginning. But how far back shall we go? The
beginning of time and the universe seems too remote to help
us, even though the miracle of creation can teach us much
about God, ourselves, and the world. The beginning of our
own lives in the womb? But that too is quite remote from our
experience, wonder and miracle though it may be. We can't
recall that moment, at least in our conscious memory.

For those who have been touched by him, life really begins
the moment when Jesus comes into our lives, the moment
when Jesus calls and we decide to follow him. The Gospels
describe men and women whose lives take a radical turn when
they are touched by Jesus and respond to him.

As a tax collector neither respected nor envied for his
wealth, Zacchaeus was thoroughly despised by his people and
excluded from synagogue worship because his occupation was
considered sinful, unclean. He hears of Jesus' approach but is
too short of stature to see him. So Zacchaeus does something
foolish—he "goes out on a limb for Christ."

Jesus looks up at Zacchaeus and invites himself to dinner in
the tax collector's house, an invitation that shocks the bystanders. The publican's life is changed, a transformation he

puts into action by promptly giving half his goods to the poor and repaying anyone he has cheated fourfold (Lk 19:1-10). Zacchaeus apparently makes a real beginning. Having been dead, he comes to life.

Or consider the woman taken in adultery (Jn 8:1-11). She lived in the prison of her own wretched self-image, barred even more securely by the attitudes and words of the professional "holy" people of the day. In Jesus this woman finally meets a man who neither exploits nor condemns her, but through the gift of forgiveness brings her to new life.

There was another woman whose encounter with Jesus was very different. It happened before she ever saw Jesus in the flesh. God asked her to be his mother! She was "troubled" by the invitation at first because she didn't understand what she was supposed to do about it. And even after the angel explained how it would happen, she had no idea what kind of future this call would bring. That's why, when she said, "Be it done to me as you say," her faith response was more perfect than the others. That's why Jesus could say of her, "Blessed are those who hear the word of God and keep it" (Lk 11:28). Her encounter with God and with Jesus now mysteriously in her womb was not, like Zacchaeus and the adulterous woman, a conversion from sin, but her life was radically and forever changed from that moment. God's call put the teenager of Nazareth on a cosmic trajectory!

ENCOUNTERING JESUS

These stories were told and retold in the early church, and thus eventually became part of our Gospels. Why were these stories so memorable? After the lightning-like moment of meeting God in faith, the lives of these people were never again the same. We see in the saints many more stories of such dramatic conversion experiences.

What about those of us who were baptized as infants, who

grew up in a Christian family, who were nourished in a faith-filled parish or Christian community? We may wonder when this sort of dramatic encounter has ever happened to us. Can you name a moment, perhaps even a particular place, which you could call your moment, your place of conversion? Was there ever a special time when you suddenly realized that the life you were leading was really not Christian, that Jesus was calling you to that kind of radical change we see in the Gospels?

It may have been during a retreat, or while reading a book, or when meeting a holy person. If there is such a moment in your life, then it is a precious moment—like a holy sanctuary in time where you are privileged to go back in your memory, take off your shoes, and rest in loving, thankful contemplation.

For others, conversion or turning to Christ may have been a gradual process, more like growing into a larger size of clothing than being hit by lightning. Perhaps you learned about Jesus from pictures in your home or church. You may have learned Bible stories from your parents or an uncle or aunt or the teachers at Sunday school or CCD. As part of a Christian community, you may have absorbed the reality of events surrounding Christmas, Good Friday, and Easter Sunday each year.

Even in this case, of course, there comes a moment when the faith of the community is not enough, when we must choose to make the faith our own, or to reject it, or simply to let it die from neglect. And this too is an important moment of growth. Perplexed by his terrible ordeal, Job listened over and over again to the answers offered by his friends—traditional answers that had sufficed for centuries. But these explanations never satisfied Job. Only when he met the Lord in his own personal experience did Job know peace. "Formerly I knew you only by hearsay, but now that my eye has seen you, I repent in dust and ashes" (Jb 42:5-6).

So, too, our faith can run only so long on the conviction of others. Sooner or later we need to make our own personal commitment to Jesus. If we have never done so, if we have always ridden piggy-back on the faith of others, then the first step is indeed an important one. We can't go anywhere unless we take that first step. We need to ask for the grace of hearing Jesus' call in our hearts and freely choosing to follow him.

In actuality, no conversion is ever total. The initial meeting of Jesus and deciding to follow him should set us on a path for the rest of our lives. But as we continue our efforts to live like a disciple, we inevitably discover that we are not so totally God's as we would like to be or once thought we were. We need to be converted again. Following the lead of St. Benedict, many speak of the Christian life as a continual conversion, a daily renewed decision to follow Jesus.

Meditations

Meeting Jesus (Jn 1:35-39); Nicodemus meets Jesus (Jn 3:1-21); the Samaritan woman meets Jesus (Jn 4:4-42); Zacchaeus (Lk 19:1-10); the woman taken in adultery (Jn 8:1-11).

FOLLOWING JESUS

After personally encountering Jesus, what does Scripture tell us about the *journey* of a disciple? What happens on the way? What does the disciple learn? How does the disciple grow?

First, the fascination of the disciples continues to grow. Who is this man who forgives sins? Who heals lepers and multiplies bread? "Who is this, that even the wind and the sea obey him?" (Mk 4:41). Peter finally receives the light to say, "You are the Messiah" (Mk 8:29). But no sooner has he made this confession than he learns that this Messiah must suffer—something Peter was not at all prepared to hear. So he must go on learning. And not until after the resurrection do Peter and the other disciples really understand that Jesus is God's only Son.

Even though we live in the shadow of the resurrection, our journey entails, no less than Peter's, daily learning of who Jesus is—for us and for the world. If married couples can spend their whole lives unwrapping the mystery of their spouse, what shall we say of the disciple who is in love with the One who is infinite mystery, God himself? If we live to be eighty, we will still be saying, "Jesus, you never cease to amaze me." Mary too followed the same journey. The angel had told her Jesus would be Israel's king, but he didn't tell her about the cross. Simeon, at the presentation of Jesus in the temple, hinted at it, but like Peter she had to hear it from Jesus' own lips. She was both mother and disciple of her Son, not fully comprehending the cross under which she stood, but also rewarded with sharing the risen glory of her Son.

We grow in the knowledge of Jesus (and of the Father whom he reveals) by prayer and the work of the Holy Spirit. We also gain insight by seeing the Lord's hand in the events of our daily lives. This knowledge becomes the first experience of growth in discipleship: "This is eternal life: to know you, the one true God, and Jesus Christ whom you have sent" (Jn 17:3).

Jesus made very clear from the beginning that following him means leaving everything. When he called the first two disciples, "they left everything and followed him" (Lk 5:11). That meant concretely that these fishermen abandoned their nets and their boats, their father and their companions (Mk 1:18-20). In short, they left their profession and their home.

The first disciples became wandering ascetics, following Jesus not only in his teaching but also in his lifestyle. They would be imitated in succeeding centuries by religious and celibate missionaries. But after the resurrection of Jesus, we see most of the growing number of disciples living in stable communities. They are lay people, most of them married, raising families and supporting themselves through their own

work. They share their goods freely with one another according to needs, but they are not "religious" in the modern sense.

No doubt they looked back on those earlier itinerant disciples with great admiration, perhaps even a holy envy. The
wandering lifestyle of Jesus symbolized the inner freedom and
total commitment of the heart which every disciple longed to
have. Not everyone was called to leave family, home, and profession. Some individuals would travel far and wide as
prophets or evangelists. And some would choose celibacy for
the sake of the kingdom (Mt 19:12). But all were called to
"seek first the kingdom of God," to hold on to that inner
freedom which flowed from tasting the glory of heaven.

GETTING INTO THE BOAT TOGETHER

Having left much behind, what does the disciple find? If we
read between the lines of the Gospels, we can well imagine the
situation of Peter and his friends. The first few days in Jesus'
company are exciting. They see people being healed, devils
being dispelled, and the crowds on the Galilean hillsides
swelling each day. This is indeed more exciting than fishing,
especially when Peter admits to having labored all night and
catching nothing.

But then Jesus does a shocking thing. Accompanied by the
four fishermen, he stops at a tax-collector's booth. *Why is Jesus
doing that?* Peter may well have asked himself. To pay the tax,
or to call Levi to repentance, perhaps even to inquire if Levi or
anyone in his family needed healing? But no. To Peter's utter
horror, Jesus tells *Levi*, "Come, follow me."

Surely, hopes Peter, *no tycoon tax collector in his right mind
would give up his lucrative profession to follow this penniless
rabbi without a home.* But wonder of wonders, Levi gets up at
once, leaves money and account books behind, and follows
Jesus. Not only follows *Jesus,* of course, but now walks at
Peter's side.

Levi was one of those people Peter could not stomach. Tax collectors were despised for collaborating with the Roman forces and for gouging people outrageously. And they were expressly forbidden entry to the synagogue. To the pious Jew tax collectors were outcasts. And now Jesus calls one of them and expects the first disciples to embrace him as a brother!

Thus begins the first episode in the unfolding story of mutual relationships. Jesus has to teach his disciples many things about how to love one another. They argue on the road about which one is greatest, wanting the first seats in the king- dom—all the while being deaf to Jesus' teachings about his own coming suffering and the cross which they all must carry (Mk 9:33-50; 10:32-45).

Jesus teaches them to become servants of one another. He teaches them to accept each other with the frankness and openness of children, to confront each other as brothers and sisters when someone has done something wrong, and above all, to forgive one another (Mt 18). At the Last Supper, Jesus prays that they may all be one (Jn 17:21), and he tells them: "By this will all people recognize you as my disciples, if you love one another" (Jn 13:35).

Thus to follow Jesus means to build community among others who follow him. In this way believers witness to Jesus more powerfully than the most eloquent sermon of a fiery preacher. In a community united in love and humble service, the world can see what heaven is like and even what God is like, since this love reflects the love in the Trinity (Jn 17:21). After Jesus' resurrection, the early disciples quickly formed communities. They knew without a doubt that one could not be a Christian alone, that community life would provide some necessary element of healthy discipleship.

These communities varied in intensity. All of them involved sharing of faith, prayer, and even a measure of material goods, but few if any adopted the lifestyle which would later charac- terize religious. But these early Christians clearly realized that Jesus had tried to form his first disciples into a community.

And they understood his efforts to apply in some way to all disciples of all times.

Jesus called his people to be a light to the world and salt for the earth (Mt 5:13-16). Yet this foretaste of heaven will not be without suffering. Indeed, the decision to be a disciple, the decision to follow Jesus, means a willingness to go with him into the storm.

The eighth chapter of Matthew describes Jesus performing three important miracles followed by an evening of healings. Crowds are pressing around him, and suddenly we find Jesus at the lakeside giving orders to cross to the other shore (Mt 8:18). Matthew does not tell us to whom he gave the orders, but lets us suspect it was to the whole crowd or to whomever would be willing to come with him.

Then we see two would-be disciples laying down conditions for following Jesus, to which he replies: "No conditions." Jesus gets into the boat first, followed by his disciples (8:23). The crowd does not follow Jesus; the disciples do. Here we see an important difference between the disciples and the crowd. It is not enough to see the miracles of Jesus or even to be cured by him. Such a person can remain wholly passive: entertained, perhaps even amazed at Jesus' power, but not really converted. To be a disciple means to get into the boat with Jesus—a boat destined for stormy seas.

The boat symbolizes the community of Jesus' disciples, the other shore its mission. Like the boat, this community is sure to encounter a violent storm. But Jesus is present and nothing else matters. As the storm intensifies the disciples awaken Jesus and ask him to do something. He first rebukes their lack of faith, then calms the storm with a verbal command.

Why rebuke their faith? Was it not an act of faith to call upon him? Perhaps. But Jesus may have wanted to teach them another lesson: how easy to believe *after* Jesus has calmed the storm, but to believe that Jesus is in the boat and that therefore we are safe *in* the midst of the storm is faith indeed—the kind of faith Christians need when their community is rocked by persecution or trials or betrayals.

The Gospels tell us little about Mary during the public life of Jesus. Some might interpret this as indicating her role was unimportant. But it is worth noting that the evangelists often intentionally create gaps, trusting the reader to fill them in. For example, the parable of the prodigal son ends without Luke telling us whether the elder son decided to enter the banquet or not. Why this omission? Because Luke wants the reader to identify with the elder son: the reader must decide to join the party or not. Similarly, one could argue that there was no need to portray constantly Mary's reaction to the events of Jesus' life. What mother, and certainly what perfect mother, could be indifferent to what was going on? Luke and John give us enough clues to her response that we can reconstruct what it was to see Jesus' public life through Mary's eyes. When Spirit-guided Christians of subsequent ages did just that, they were merely filling in the gap left by the evangelists. Looking at each step in Jesus' journey through Mary's eyes gives us an understanding of her own faith journey. As the model disciple of her Son, she also helps us respond with a deeper faith of the heart.

Meditations

Look up and meditate on the Scripture references given in the last two sections above.

CELEBRATING OUR UNION WITH JESUS

Faith is the personal relationship that comes from meeting Jesus and accepting him as our Lord and Savior. Jesus is the foundation of our entire spiritual life. "No other foundation can be laid than the one already laid, Jesus Christ" (1 Cor 3:11). Therefore, to say that Jesus is the foundation and that faith is the foundation amounts to the same thing. The Council of Trent put it this way: "Faith is the beginning, the foundation, and the root of all justification."

As we grow in the knowledge of Jesus, we will find that he leads us to know the Father and to desire and work for the kingdom. To do this he gives us the Holy Spirit. But all this happens because we first meet and accept Jesus and decide to follow him.

The decision to follow Jesus means leaving some things and finding others. We leave our securities and our own way of doing things to learn his ways. We find and accept his word, his teaching, and we try to live by it. We also accept the company of other disciples, which sometimes seems a lot harder than accepting Jesus! And we are ready to go with Jesus and his disciples into the unknown future, even into a storm.

The early Christians celebrated this union with Jesus in a unique way: baptism, which also involved an anointing or laying on of hands, later called confirmation. And then they celebrated the Eucharist for the first time. These are called the sacraments of initiation: the external ritualization of what happens when we meet Jesus. And because our meeting with Jesus is not something we dreamed up on our own but rather the pure gift of God's grace, these sacraments are actually the external sign of God's conferring on us this new life, this covenant union with Jesus.

Every new step forward in our discipleship is in some way the awakening of our baptismal grace. When we celebrate the high-point of our faith at the Easter Vigil, we renew our baptismal promises and recall our baptism by the sprinkling of holy water. No valid spirituality exists apart from that already given by Christ to the church. By getting in touch with the grace of our baptism, we become more deeply consecrated to God. To be holy means to become what we are by our baptism, which we will explore in the next chapter.

Steps on the Journey

1. How have you experienced conversion in your life? Suddenly? Gradually?

2. When did you first become aware that you were called to make a personal commitment to Jesus? What kind of changes in your lifestyle do you need to make in order to live this commitment on a daily basis?

3. In what specific areas can you become more "community conscious" and follow Jesus better in your social relationships: with spouse, children, in-laws, extended family, friends, co-workers, fellow parishioners, or community members?

4. What material possessions or habits do you need to leave behind to continue your journey to Jesus? What new attitudes or ways of looking at situations or responding to circumstances do you need to find?

5. What are some practical ways you can daily renew your commitment to Jesus? What role does faith play in doing so? How can Mary help you respond in faith to the daily call of Jesus?

Lord Jesus, I want you to be the Lord of my life. I want to surrender everything to you and to follow you. I accept the conditions of discipleship, and I welcome the community of brothers and sisters, the concrete expression of your church in my life. But I need ever deeper conversion. Grant me the grace to respond to your call today and to let go of those things in my life that hold me back from running after you with a full heart. Mary, teach me how to see Jesus through your eyes. Amen.

THREE

Becoming a
New Creation

WE ARE CONSECRATED THROUGH BAPTISM and receive the gift of the Spirit. Baptism is not just the beginning of our life in Christ, it is also the end. We see in the sacrament of baptism not only what we have become but also what we ultimately are meant to be: totally God's, a new creation (2 Cor 5:17).

The early church taught new converts the meaning of this sacrament by contemplating the baptism of Jesus in the Jordan. To find out what happened to us in our baptism and what we are to become, we too need to look at the baptism of Jesus. According to the Gospel of Mark, "It happened in those days that Jesus came from Nazareth of Galilee and was baptized in the Jordan by John. On coming up out of the water he saw the heavens being torn open and the Spirit, like a dove, descending upon him. And a voice came from the heavens, 'You are my beloved Son; with you I am well pleased'" (Mk 1:9-11, NAB).

Why should Jesus undergo John's baptism, which was a baptism of repentance? Christ willingly submitted not to repent of his own sins but to repent for ours. Our baptism is also a baptism of repentance, which explains why the *renewal* of baptismal promises begins with a renunciation of sin, Satan, and his works. It also explains why the sacrament of reconciliation is important for anyone who wishes to renew his or her baptismal covenant. We go down into the waters of repentance with Jesus and claim for ourselves the repentance he has already made for our sins.

But then Jesus came up out of the water; and what happened then also happens to us in our baptism. *First, the heavens are opened.* We now have access to God, to the divine throne room. We are welcomed into the intimate life of the Trinity. We can now call God "Abba," dearest Father, because he has opened his heart to us and welcomed us in.

Second, the Holy Spirit is given to us. The dove over the waters of baptism recalls the hovering of God's spirit over the waters of the first creation, as well as the dove that returned to Noah at the time of the flood to announce the beginning of a new world. In baptism the Holy Spirit makes of us something brand new—a new creation (2 Cor 5:17). The Holy Spirit makes us cry out "Abba," and helps us experience the fatherly embrace of God (Gal 4:6; Rom 8:15). The Holy Spirit brings many fruits such as love, joy, and peace (Gal 5:22), along with gifts that invite and impel us to build up the church. In short, the Holy Spirit conforms us to Jesus in his relationship with his Father and in his mission to the world.

Third, the Father tells us we are his beloved. He delights in us as a human father delights in his newborn child. We often forget what astounding good news this is. "There is now no condemnation for those who are in Christ Jesus" (Rom 8:1). Nor should there be any *self*-condemnation either. If God loves us as his dearest children, does anything else really matter?

BAPTISMAL GRACE AND MISSION

John the Baptist proclaimed Jesus as more powerful because he would baptize with the Holy Spirit rather than water (Mk 1:7-8). The Spirit that comes upon Jesus in his baptism anoints him for public ministry (Lk 4:18). Empowered by the Holy Spirit, Jesus preaches, heals, casts out demons, and offers his life for the redemption of the world (see Heb 9:13-14). If baptism makes us children of God and puts God's love in our hearts, does the Holy Spirit also anoint us for ministry?

Most certainly! It is not for ourselves alone that God works his wonders, but for building up the new people of God and bringing about God's kingdom on earth. To put it plainly, the Holy Spirit makes us missionaries. But we are missionaries first by sharing our faith with our brothers and sisters in the Christian community for mutual upbuilding. In fact, the Holy Spirit gives specific gifts for the upbuilding of the community in faith and love.

If we survey the gifts of the Spirit mentioned in 1 Corinthians 12-14 and elsewhere, we find that the Holy Spirit transforms those he touches in the following ways.

Praise transforms our tongues. The Holy Spirit caused Jesus to rejoice and praise the Father (Lk 10:21). And when the Holy Spirit came upon the disciples in the upper room, he transformed them into a community of jubilant praise (Acts 2:11). Genuine praise is not just saying the right words, nor merely singing them out of routine. The Spirit's gift of praise wells up from the heart like a fountain and always exceeds what words could express.

When the Holy Spirit came upon Mary, she not only conceived Jesus in her womb. She was empowered to burst forth in jubilant praise in her Magnificat.

True praise is like the emotion I once felt when I was a missionary in Nepal. After our group had trekked through valleys for three days, we topped a ridge and were suddenly confronted by the snow-capped Himalayan splendor of twenty-six-thousand-foot Daulagiri. "Breath-taking" would be a major understatement for the experience.

One of the manifestations of this gift of praise mentioned in the New Testament is the gift of tongues, a praise of God that goes from the heart to the tongue without passing through the mind. It may sound like a jumble of syllables, but this strange language provides a way of saying that our God is too big for any human words to contain him, that only the language of the heart (or of the spirit) can approach the mystery. Tongues is a prayer language that is submerged in God. When the disciples were caught up in this kind of praise on Pentecost, bystanders thought they were drunk.[1]

Hearing transforms our ears. A second gift which normally follows the gift of intense praise is the gift of hearing. This gift of ears concerns not physical hearing, but spiritual hearing—that is, the ability to really hear God speaking, to hear a "word from the Lord." The Bible refers to this as the gift of prophecy.

Prophecy doesn't mean the ability to foretell the future. If it means speaking a word from the Lord, it implies first that the person hears the Lord's word in his or her heart. This hearing does not just repeat some text of Scripture from the past; it is a word with a here-and-now meaning. Even if it does repeat something scriptural, the prophetic word has a fresh meaning for the present situation. "Morning after morning he opens my ear," says the prophet (Is 50:4, NAB).

Can you remember a prayer or retreat experience when a word of the Lord came crashing into your mind and heart? Perhaps it came in such a way that you felt God speaking personally to you, touching you so powerfully that it changed your life. That was an experience of the gift of prophecy. We can develop this precious gift of the Holy Spirit by prayer and an expectant listening. "Speak, Lord, for your servant is listening" (1 Sm 3:10).

Healing and service anoints our hands. We also see the gift of healing working in Jesus and in the early Christian community. Jesus touches people and they are healed; the early Christians lay hands on the sick and they get well. This gift of healing prayer is given to all of us through the Holy Spirit.[2] It must be awakened by asking for it and then developed through practice. The next time someone who is sick asks you to pray for them, resist the usual response, "Yes, I will." Seize the opportunity and say instead, "May I pray with you right now?"

When my brother Frank was two years old, he overturned a kettle of boiling water on himself. He was so badly burned that the doctors said only a skin graft could repair the damage. A neighbor had already volunteered to supply the skin. That night my aunt prayed fervently for Frank, pouring some Lourdes water onto his burns. The next morning my brother's skin was amazingly restored, to the astonishment of all, including the doctors.

Many other gifts of the Spirit can be classified under gifts of service. Giving ourselves in humble service to our brothers and sisters allows God's love to flow through us. The spiritual gift of service stands in stark contrast to work which is anxious, burdened, or done with carelessness or indifference. Service rendered by godly strength conveys joy and a sense of God's presence and love (1 Pt 4:11). When Jesus washed the feet of his disciples, he touched much more than their feet. Each one of them would remember that humble gesture as a sign of how perfectly Jesus loved them (Jn 13:1). No doubt he had learned this kind of service in the home at Nazareth from the one who described herself as the Lord's servant (Lk 1:38). She had also communicated the good news to Elizabeth not only in her Magnificat of praise but in her service to her cousin in need.

Evangelization gives wings to our feet. When the Holy Spirit fell upon the disciples gathered in the upper room, timid souls were transformed into bold missionaries (Acts 2). The Holy Spirit makes each one he touches into a missionary. No sooner do we receive the Spirit than we feel a burning desire to share the gift with others.

No sooner had the Holy Spirit conceived Jesus in the

womb of Mary than she got up and went with haste to share the good news with her cousin Elizabeth. The outpouring of the Holy Spirit upon Jesus in his baptism made him the first bringer of good news from village to village (Lk 4:14, 18-19).

Thus we can call this gift of the Spirit the gift of feet, beautiful feet like those of Jesus and Mary, traveling to bring the good news to others. "How beautiful upon the mountains are the feet of the messenger who brings good news, who announces peace" (Is 52:7).

FANNING THE FLAME

But you may object, I don't really experience my life this way. How do I activate the grace of my baptism? And even if I have experienced moments of such intimacy, how do I lay hold of the God who is always offering us "more than we can ask or imagine" (Eph 3:20)?

When we consider the gifts of the Spirit, we may respond with guilt: "If I hadn't done that," or "If I were a better person, then I might experience God's closeness more." Obviously, if we are conscious of serious sin or a sinful attachment in our lives, we ought to repent of it and ask forgiveness. But our guilt may be based on the false assumption that God's gift is a reward for our holiness, which replays the old heresy of Pelagianism.

This merit-reward approach comes more from our upbringing and our worldly experience than it does from Scripture. One or both of our parents may have given us the impression that if we were good they would love us, and if we were bad they wouldn't. Perhaps from the early days of school onward, we knew that only hard work won gold stars and promotions.

Whenever we made a mistake, we may have been put down by someone who would tell us something like, "You'll never amount to anything," "You're always screwing up," "You're never on time"—all of which convinced us that we were really not good people. These tapes recorded in our memory make it all the more difficult to hear the fresh voice of God which whispers, "I love you as my dearest child, and I delight in you."

So how do we get those tapes erased? By letting the Holy Spirit and God's word to us wipe them out. But how do we do that? Simple. We ask for it. Jesus promised that we need only sincerely ask for the Holy Spirit and it will happen: "And I tell you, ask and you will receive; seek and you will find; knock and the door will be opened to you. For everyone who asks, receives; and the one who seeks, finds; and to the one who knocks, the door will be opened. What father among you would hand his son a snake when he asks for a fish? Or hand him a scorpion when he asks for an egg? If you then... know how to give good gifts to your children, *how much more will the Father in heaven give the Holy Spirit to those who ask him?*" (Lk 11:9-13, NAB; emphasis mine).

This sort of asking cannot be done casually. We need to pray fervently and with great expectation, an activity which expands our capacity to receive. St. Thomas Aquinas believed that the reason God wants us to ask and to keep on asking is so that our capacity will be as great as the gifts he longs to give us.

The early church and its ministers realized that the grace received in an earlier sacrament may need to be "fanned into flame." The author of 2 Timothy writes: "I am reminding you now to fan into a flame the gift that God gave you when I laid my hands on you. God's gift was not a spirit of timidity, but the Spirit of power, and love, and self-control" (2 Tm 1:6-7).

TRANSFORMED BY THE HOLY SPIRIT

Once we have yielded to the Holy Spirit, it is important to let him take over our lives, for it is his role to transform us into the image of Christ himself: "We all, with faces unveiled, reflecting as in a mirror the glory of the Lord, are being transformed into that very image, in a way that only the Lord can do, who is the Spirit" (2 Cor 3:18).

Thus the life in the Spirit involves a process of growth, in which we seek ever more deeply the divine love which bears fruit in joy, patience, long-suffering, and the other fruits of the Spirit (Gal 5:22), and the gifts that allow the Holy Spirit to use us as instruments in building up the body of Christ. We enter into a process of growing in holiness, which means "consecration." Paul prays that his readers be thoroughly consecrated: "May the God of peace consecrate you through and through, and may your whole being, spirit, soul, and body, be preserved blameless for the coming of our Lord Jesus Christ" (1 Thes 5:23).

Growing in holiness or belonging to God is a process that continues until the Lord comes again. Consecrating a chalice or a church withdraws it from common use and sets it aside for the service of God. A chalice or a church cannot "grow in holiness." But human beings can. Our baptismal consecration not only puts us in a state of belonging to God in a once-done act but also initiates a lifelong process of "becoming what we are."

But how do we cooperate with the Holy Spirit's ongoing formation of us? I would suggest two intimately united ways: one is symbol, the other is system. The *symbol* is Mary, who perfectly cooperated with the Holy Spirit in all he wished to do in her and through her. She is the one from whom we can learn, intuitively as it were, how to follow the Spirit's lead.

The *system* is a step-by-step learning of the virtues which gradually transform us into the likeness of Christ. Basically this combination builds on the Old Testament wisdom tradition, such as we find in Proverbs, Sirach, and the Wisdom of Solomon, where Wisdom is personified as a woman who instructs her children in the practical ways of holiness. Wisdom is a woman and a way. To this woman and her way we now turn.

Exercises

- Meditate on the scene of Jesus' baptism and prayerfully reflect that his baptism is also your baptism. Renew your experience by seeing yourself descend into the Jordan waters of repentance with Jesus. Then see yourself coming up and knowing in faith that you have been admitted to the throne room of your Father. Now open yourself to the gift of the Holy Spirit and ask to be empowered with a specific gift: praise, hearing God's word, healing, or the fruits of the Spirit mentioned in Galatians 5:22.

- Make a novena to the Holy Spirit, in union with Mary, to ask for a greater outpouring of the Holy Spirit and his gifts in your life.

- Make a retreat geared specifically to asking for the grace of the Holy Spirit to renew your life. Many charismatic prayer groups offer a "Life in the Spirit" seminar which leads the participants through themes such as the love of God, salvation, new life, openness to God's gift, and then climaxes with the laying on of hands and praying for the release of the Holy Spirit.

Steps on the Journey

1. Can you think of some gift you didn't realize you had until much later in your life? How does this compare with the gift of your baptism?

2. What experiences have you already had of spiritual renewal (perhaps a new awareness of being a child of God, or a new perception of your uniqueness in God's eyes)? How has your attitude toward your baptism (if you were baptized as an infant or a young person) changed now that you're an adult?

3. Have you been tempted to be satisfied with your past level of spiritual life? Why is this a dangerous option?

4. How have you experienced the gift of praise—in groups, at liturgies or services at your church, or when attending a wedding or funeral? Are you open to the fact that people praise God in different ways than you?

5. How can you be more open to Mary's counsel and example as you pray about what your baptism really means to you? What do these symbols of Mary mean to you: mother, woman, teacher, counselor, and guide? Think of some other words to describe her influence in your life.

6. What does the phrase "to hear the Lord's words in one's heart" really mean to you? Have you ever experienced that kind of hearing? When you listen to the readings and prayers during liturgies, do you listen for God's personal word to you?

Heavenly Father, I thank you for all that you have given to me in baptism. I thank you for joining me to Jesus' baptism and making me your beloved son/daughter. I thank you for the gift of your love, which is the Person of the Holy Spirit. Renew the power of that Holy Spirit in me, anoint me once more in the depth of my being, so that I may become wholly yours and, like Mary, be your instrument for bringing Jesus to the world. Amen.

FOUR

The Gift of Mary

JUST AS TODAY, the early church baptized people who were far from perfect. The rite of their baptismal consecration was followed by what they called *mystagogia*, which entailed elaborate instruction on what had happened in their initiation and the kind of life that should flow from it. The newly baptized were expected to live up to the title which they bore, "saints," which means "consecrated people." The church continues a form of this *mystagogia* in the Rite of Christian Initiation of Adults (RCIA), which is the initiations process for adults in parishes today.

Paul offers an example of this kind of post-baptismal instruction in his letter to the Ephesians:

> [Y]ou must no longer live as the Gentiles do, in the futility of their minds; darkened in understanding, alienated from the life of God because of their ignorance, because of their hardness of heart, they have become callous and have handed themselves over to licentiousness for the practice of every kind of impurity to excess. That is not how you learned Christ, assuming that you have heard of him and were taught in him, as truth is in Jesus, that you should *put*

away the old self of your former way of life, corrupted
through deceitful desires, and *be renewed in the spirit of your
minds, and put on the new self,* created in God's way in
righteousness and holiness of truth.

Therefore, putting away falsehood, speak the truth, each
one to his neighbor, for we are members one of another. Be
angry but do not sin; do not let the sun set on your anger,
and do not leave room for the devil.... No foul language
should come out of your mouths, but only such as is good
for needed edification, that it may impart grace to those
who hear. And do not grieve the Holy Spirit of God, with
which you were sealed for the day of redemption. All bitterness, fury, anger, shouting, and reviling must be removed
from you, along with all malice. [And] be kind to one
another, compassionate, forgiving one another as God has
forgiven you in Christ. Ephesians 4:17-32, NAB; emphasis mine

The sacred author uses several images: putting off the old
self and putting on the new, the exhortation to be renewed in
mind, learning to control one's emotions, and especially
guarding one's speech. A little further on, he wraps all of this
into a symbol: the church as a woman, the bride of Christ,
"consecrated and cleansed by the bath of water with the word,
that he [Christ] might present to himself the church in all her
splendor, without spot or wrinkle or anything like it, that she
might be holy and without stain" (Eph 5:26-27).

Notice, therefore, that the program for the post-baptismal
church is not merely a *system;* it is also a *symbol.* As Christian
tradition developed, it became clear that the symbol of perfect
baptismal consecration was no longer a metaphorical woman.
The ultimate perfection of the church, the bride of Christ,
already existed in a real woman of history. It was Mary, mother
of Jesus and model of perfect discipleship and of all the virtues.

Mary is the woman of wisdom who shows us the way of
wisdom. Hence, to arrive more quickly and surely to the holiness already mapped out by our baptismal consecration, what

better way than to put ourselves in the company of the woman who not only embodies the church's ultimate holiness but also can teach us how to get there. This entrustment came to be called "consecration to Mary."

CONSECRATION TO MARY

The one most known for promoting the practice of consecration to Mary is St. Louis Grignion de Montfort, whose book, *True Devotion to Mary*, is a Catholic classic. It powerfully influenced the spiritual life of Pope John Paul II, even inspiring his motto, *Totus tuus*, "All yours."

Although he lived a century before Fr. Chaminade, de Montfort's manuscript was not discovered until 1842, when Fr. Chaminade was eighty-one years old. So Chaminade's spirituality of consecration had developed quite independently of de Montfort's. Though different in application, they both reflect a common source. And, most importantly, they both consider consecration to Mary to be a way of making more real and effective one's baptismal consecration. Thus Grignion de Montfort says:

As all perfection consists in our being conformed, united and consecrated to Jesus it naturally follows that the most perfect of all devotions is that which conforms, unites, and consecrates us most completely to Jesus. Now of all God's creatures Mary is the most conformed to Jesus. It therefore follows that, of all devotions, devotion to her makes for the most effective consecration and conformity to him. The more one is consecrated to Mary, the more one is consecrated to Jesus.... It is the perfect renewal of the vows and promises of holy baptism.[1]

Fr. Chaminade used the renewal of baptismal promises as the first stage of admission to the Marian Sodality, the final stage being an act of consecration to Mary. He stressed the notion of filiation, a son or daughter relationship to Mary, rather than the "holy slavery" promoted by de Montfort. Fr. Chaminade also considered consecration to Mary to have a horizontal, corporate dimension, in the sense that consecration also bound one ever more deeply to the Christian community of which one was a part. Thus his notion of consecration perfectly reflected baptismal consecration, which encompassed both a belonging to God and to the church.

To allow the Holy Spirit the fullest freedom to transform us, the first step is to entrust ourselves to Mary. But this step should not be taken lightly. A profound spiritual preparation must precede it. Because this consecration to Mary is so foundational to the program of spiritual growth outlined in this book, you will benefit from the following instruction and background material. The reader's patience in undertaking this theological detour will be amply rewarded.

MARY, GIFT OF THE HOLY SPIRIT

Jesus was formed in the womb of Mary by the action of the Holy Spirit, a truth on which Fr. Chaminade dwelt at length. From it he drew the consequence that every Christian must also be formed "in the womb of her maternal tenderness" until the image of Jesus is fully achieved. Such a leap of logic may not be fully obvious from Scripture. Yet it corresponds to the broader hints given in the New Testament that Mary is a gift both of Jesus and the Holy Spirit, and that as such she plays a modeling and mothering role in our lives.[2]

Jesus assured his disciples that the Holy Spirit would teach them everything and remind them of all that Jesus had said (Jn 14:26). And Paul writes, "We have not received the spirit of the world but the Spirit from God, so that we may *understand* the things that have been given us by God" (1 Cor 2:12, emphasis mine). Thus the Holy Spirit will bring to life in our experience the full mystery of Jesus, what he taught and lived. He will interpret what Jesus means for us here and now.

In the Last Supper discourse, Jesus goes on to say that the Spirit can fulfill that role because "he will take from what is mine and declare it to you" (Jn 16:15).

Now what belongs to Jesus? What "things of his" will the Spirit bring alive in us? His Father; his Word; the mysteries of his life (birth, passion, death, resurrection, and the various events of his public life related in the Gospels); the sacraments of baptism and the Eucharist, his own flesh and blood; his disciples, whom Jesus calls his "own" (Jn 17:6-10); and one of his most precious gifts, his mother.

Mary is not only the way God's Son became one of us in the mystery of the incarnation. She is not only given to us as an example of faith. Jesus explicitly gives her to us at the climactic moment of his life, on Calvary, when he said to the beloved disciple, "There is your mother" (Jn 19:25-27). Mary is the woman of Genesis 3:15 whose offspring will overcome the serpent. She is also the embodiment of Mother Jerusalem, bringing forth the new generation of God's children, represented by the beloved disciple.[3]

We read at the conclusion of the Calvary scene: "And from that hour the disciple took her into his home." The Greek literally means, "The disciple welcomed her into the things that were his own." He *welcomed* her. The evangelist has just proclaimed, in a subtle way, that the new birth of the people of God has taken place. Mary is not only mother of the Savior on the cross. She is now mother of the disciples. And the beloved disciple is a model disciple in welcoming her.

The Gospels are filled with examples of persons who remained obtuse to the gifts Jesus offered, or even rejected them. Even some of his own disciples left him when he offered them the Eucharist (Jn 6:66). But the beloved disciple proves to be keenly aware of the preciousness of this gift: "Jesus has made his own mother my mother!" The disciple takes her into the things *that were his own*, that is, into the treasury of his heart.

We too are invited to welcome Mary as the beloved disciple

did. That, briefly, is what consecration to Mary is really about. We do not consecrate ourselves to Mary as if she were God. We simply open ourselves to the gift Jesus and the Holy Spirit offer to us of Mary as our mother. We consciously and with deep gratitude accept and welcome her. And whenever we recognize and accept any of the gifts of God, we are more deeply consecrated to God.

Have you ever consciously received Mary as your mother? Have you ever consciously said yes to this gift? Far from being a threat to Jesus, when you receive his gifts, you receive him in a deeper way. If you would like to experience the gift of Mary and receive her from Jesus, you might find the following prayer of consecration helpful:

Lord Jesus,
You gave Mary, your mother,
To the disciple whom you loved
As your final gift before you died,
That she should be his mother and mine.
As the beloved disciple took her to be his own,
So I now take her as my mother.
Under her influence may I be formed
By the Holy Spirit to your likeness
And proclaim the gift you continue to make of her
For the building up of your body, the church,
To the glory of God the Father. Amen.[4]

Fr. Chaminade taught his disciples to renew their consecration by pausing daily at three o'clock to recall the death of Jesus on Calvary and to enter into the mystery of Jesus' gift of his mother to the church and to each of us. Living our consecration demands a certain awareness. A daily renewal of our consecration, especially at the hour of salvation, provides one of the best ways.

When I was teaching at the Franciscan University of Steubenville, I had an afternoon class which ran from two fifteen to three thirty. Each day at three o'clock I would hear the beeping of a watch. One of my students who was enthusiastic about Sr. Faustina's devotion to the divine mercy was reminding himself to pause for a moment to recall the hour of salvation.

Although Fr. Chaminade did not write any particular formula for the three o'clock prayer, one was soon fashioned. Today's version goes something like this:

> Lord Jesus, we gather in spirit at the foot of the cross with your mother and the disciple whom you loved. We ask your pardon for our sins which are the cause of your death. We thank you for remembering us in that hour of salvation and for giving us Mary as our mother. Holy Virgin, take us under your protection and open us to the action of the Holy Spirit.
>
> St. John, obtain for us the grace of taking Mary into our life, as you did, and of assisting her in her mission. May the Father and the Son and the Holy Spirit be glorified in all places through the Immaculate Virgin Mary. Amen.

IN THE SCHOOL OF MARY

Once we have consecrated ourselves to Mary, we must strive to let the Holy Spirit use her to form us spiritually. How do we go about this? Imagine, if you will, the Holy Spirit as a sculptor. We are the stone he is trying to shape into Jesus.

In this case, the stone is actually a living being, capable of consciously cooperating in the sculptor's action. While he is working on us, we should keep our eyes fixed on Jesus, our model. What we see in Jesus is what the Spirit is trying to form in us: his attitudes, his love, his joy, his peace, his dream of the Father's kingdom on earth, his total dedication to the Father and to the work of the kingdom, and so forth.

But one member of our race has already gone through this same experience of transformation: Mary. From her we can intuitively learn how to respond to the action of the Holy Spirit. Jesus was formed in her by the action of the Holy

Spirit. With her, in her company, and with her help, we will find Jesus being formed in us.

Mary will show us how to believe "all that the Lord has promised" and thus enable the Holy Spirit to accomplish the fullness of his wonders in us. She will show us how to hope even when we feel enveloped by the darkness of Calvary.

Above all, Mary's motherly tenderness will help us to see not only God's tender love for us but the compassionate love we should have for others. After all, Jesus first learned compassion from his own mother! If we contemplate Jesus through the eyes of Mary, seeing the Gospel scenes with her faith and learning to respond with her, we will find a depth of meaning otherwise unavailable.

If this sounds a bit complicated, it is so only in theory and not in experience. When we first learn about the Holy Trinity, we can find it terribly confusing to think of Three as being One. And to add Mary to the picture seems to complicate it even more. But our confusion stems from the fact that we haven't grasped the essential role of God's love, which is the Holy Spirit.

The Holy Spirit is the spirit of relationships. First, he is the primary relationship between Father and Son in the Trinity. The Holy Spirit is produced like current by the whirling dynamo of the Father loving the Son and the Son loving the Father. The Eastern church considers the Holy Spirit the dance of the Father and Son, which some liturgies dramatize by having the eucharistic celebrants dance around the altar. A dance calls for more dancers. The Holy Spirit reaches out and takes us into the dance, just as he first reached out and took Mary into the dance. If we hold her hand and watch her steps, we will learn the dance quickly. And we can catch the hands of others and sweep them into the dance.

We can grow in our understanding of Mary and our devotion to her in many ways. Christians have used certain practices for centuries, like the rosary, novenas, and pilgrimages. But Mary's role is especially fruitful in our prayer time. Ask her presence and intercession as you begin to pray. And as you contemplate Jesus, ask to be able to see him through his mother's eyes. Leave the graces you receive in prayer in her hands.

As you wrestle with the challenges of the virtues outlined in this book, ask Mary to be with you. The journey is a lot easier—and quicker!—with her at your side. I remember inviting my novices to do a meditation exercise about the story of Jesus and his disciples crossing the lake in a storm. I invited them in their imagination to get into the boat with Jesus, to experience the storm and the waves and the near-sinking vessel, to approach Jesus as the disciples did in panic, and so forth. After twenty minutes we each shared our experiences. One by one they told of their imaginary faith journey with Jesus—how they reacted to the storm, their struggle to trust Jesus, and so on. The last novice to share surprised everyone.

He said, "You told us we should always begin our prayer with Mary, so I did. I invited her into the boat with us. And we set off. We kept sailing and sailing and sailing. I was waiting for the storm, but before I knew it we had safely landed on the other shore. Sorry, but I missed the storm!"

Mary certainly doesn't shelter us from all storms. She, after all, went through the worst one at the foot of the cross. But this novice's story does confirm a point made by St. Bernard, St. Louis Grignion de Montfort, and other saints: with Mary we face fewer storms and reach the port more rapidly and safely. If we are aware of the presence of Mary in our journey through the virtues, the pilgrimage will be not only more fruitful but more delightful!

THE SOCIAL DIMENSION OF MARIAN CONSECRATION

In reviewing the scriptural background, we saw how the woman was an image for a collectivity—Jerusalem, the people of God, the church. And we saw that Mary is the perfect embodiment of that collectivity, the community of the church. We cannot, therefore, really accept Mary into our lives without at the same time accepting the Christian community.

If Marian consecration involves a deepening of our baptismal consecration, then the ecclesial dimension of baptism must appear as well. In baptism we are not only joined to the Holy Trinity, we are anointed for service to the church and to the world. We are called to mission. So, too, with our Marian consecration.

This social dimension can be expressed in many different ways. In Fr. Chaminade's view, the church is meant to become the family of Mary. When we join ourselves to others who share the same inspiration and desire, we hope to create a model for what the whole church could become. Thus, belonging to some community in the church, especially with others who have made the Marian consecration, is an essential dimension of the consecration. As dedication to a common mission flows from that belonging, we become the apostolic family of Mary.

Exercises

- Make a Marian consecration. This means entrusting your entire life, your bodily and spiritual goods to her: *Totus tuus*. Use the consecration prayer given in this chapter or compose your own. Renew this consecration daily.

- Say the three o'clock prayer daily. Use the formula given above, or make up your own.

- In prayer, ask Jesus to reveal his mother to you.

- When you begin your prayer time, try keeping an image of Mary at hand. Ask for her presence and intercession as you begin your prayer. If you are contemplating a Gospel scene, do so through the eyes of Mary. Notice what a difference this "lens" makes in your prayer.

- Join with others who have the same desire for apostolic consecration, and let Mary be the inspiration of the group.

Steps on the Journey

1. The boy Jesus was formed by Mary in the virtues and habits of a holy family. How can your response to your baptismal call and your commitment to Jesus be assisted by a personal relationship with Mary?

2. As you prayerfully reflect on the scriptural references given above and the biblical imagery, how do you see Mary challenging you to live your relationship with God, with your family, with your associates and colleagues, with your friends and acquaintances?

3. How do you approach Mary? Try to imagine some Gospel scene in which you see yourself sitting or standing next to Mary. What difference does this make?

4. What are some of the benefits that might result from a personal consecration to Mary?

Prayer: Use the Marian consecration on page 58 or the three o'clock prayer on page 59.

FIVE

Faith of the Heart

I MAGINE CLIMBING a steep and winding mountain path, with your best friend a few minutes ahead of you. You come to a split in the pathway and puzzle over which one to take. Your friend shouts down to you, "Take the path to the left."

The one to the right seems less obstructed and more inviting, but you trust your friend's judgment. After all, that person is your friend and has a better view of the terrain from above. Despite evidence to the contrary, you choose the path your friend recommends.

This decision would be called an *act of faith*. It consists of two distinct elements: first, the *what* of your act of faith, the object, the statement; second, the *who* of your act of faith, the person in whom you believe. The what in this case is your friend's instruction to take the path to the left; the who is your trusted friend. Because of your friend's advice, you accept and act on something that is not wholly obvious from your point of view.

Faith in the Lord is like that. The what or object of faith can change according to the need of the moment, just as your friend might later tell you, "Watch out for that slippery rock ahead." The *what* of faith involves three primary issues: God's Word, God's care, and God's power. But the *who* remains constant: God himself. We trust him because we know he is God, he is truth itself, he loves us with an infinite love, and he tells us only what is good for us.

Whenever we make an act of faith in the Lord, we thereby meet him in our trust, deepen our relationship, and solidify our union. To exercise our faith is always to grow in our love of the Lord, to come closer to him. By its very nature, faith is a union with God himself. Even when we aren't conscious of his presence within us, faith assures us of God's indwelling. "May Christ dwell in your hearts through faith" (Eph 3:17).

If Jesus is there, then all his riches are there too. "We have in us the fountain of all graces, Jesus Christ, who resides within us and belongs to us; and we have the means of drawing from this source. This means is faith. What immense treasures we have in Jesus Christ! We unite ourselves to Jesus Christ by the faith we have in him; we draw from these treasures by this faith, since these treasures are ours."[1] St. Paul expressed this same faith when he proclaimed, "I can do all things in him who strengthens me" (Phil 4:13).

REVELATIONAL FAITH IN GOD'S WORD

God reveals himself to us in his Word—the Word of Scripture as preached and taught by the church. We learn who he is through the events described in that Word: the call; the covenants; the promise of a Savior; the fulfillment of that promise in the life, death, and resurrection of Jesus; and the sending of the Holy Spirit.

If we read or listen to this Word only out of idle curiosity, intellectual analysis, or momentary entertainment, we will profit no more than reading a magazine in the same spirit. But if we read or listen to Scripture as a personal message of God addressed to us, then we are listening with *revelational* faith.

Repeating a statement of faith helps us to grow in faith. For example, suppose I read the words of Jesus, "I am the way, the truth, and the life." Then I repeat those words slowly and lovingly and say, "Jesus, I believe you are the way, you are the truth, you are the life." I consider how different my life would be if I really believed that truth with all my heart and soul. And I ask the grace to believe that truth more deeply: "I do believe, Lord, increase my faith."

Our personal prayer offers the privileged time for repeating such acts of faith, but I encourage you to do so throughout the day. Our thinking or self-talk can contribute to healthy emotions. If we constantly let our mind be flooded with God's truth, we will feel happier and our behavior will change for the better.

In centuries past, when very few people owned a Bible or even a New Testament, Christians used the prayer-summary of the Scriptures which they knew by heart, the Creed. They learned to meditate on each phrase, to repeat acts of faith in it, and to apply it to their lives. This would still be a helpful practice of faith for us in our prayer time, especially when we don't have a copy of the Scriptures at hand, while walking or traveling, for example.

Exercises

- Begin with your favorite passage of Scripture. When a particular phrase strikes you, pause, and say, "Lord, I do believe your word to me.... Increase my faith." Then repeat the phrase slowly, over and over, as long as you find fruit in it, periodically repeating your acts of faith.

- Say the Creed slowly and whenever a phrase attracts you, repeat it with your lips over and over again (for example, "I believe in Jesus... who was born of the Virgin Mary") and let it slowly penetrate your heart, and soon it will transform your life.

PROVIDENTIAL FAITH IN GOD'S CARE

God also speaks to us in the events of our lives. God can use powerful occasions to move our hearts and even our wills to action: perhaps the death of a parent or friend, meeting a saintly person, living with someone who has cancer, or serving the poor. But God can also speak in the ordinary events of every day: the clouds, the mountains, the fields, the birds, our everyday duties, the people with whom we live or work.

He is the God of surprises and the God of rhythms, the God of paschal time and the God of ordinary time. To see the Lord in each of these events is a great grace. To see his loving hand in the chain of events of our past years is an even greater grace—especially to see our lives, like that of God's people in the Old Testament, as a history of salvation. We come to believe in a God who cares for us: "Look at the birds: they do not plant seeds or gather a harvest into barns; yet your Father in heaven feeds them! Aren't you worth much more than birds? Can any of you lengthen your life by worrying about it?" (Mt 6:26-27).

To see our Father's hand in the good things that happen may not be so difficult. To see that same hand in the painful things, the crosses that come our way, is the grace of a greater faith. It was the kind of faith St. Paul had. Read Romans 8:28-39, and note especially the line: "For those who love God, he makes all things work together unto good...." If we live by faith in God's love, nothing really harmful can ever happen to us. Even a violent death is victory because of him who loved us.[2] We need this kind of faith not only for our personal lives but for the life and mission of our church and our community. Father Chaminade reflects on this truth:

Faith consists in seeing God in all things; to see him in the person of superiors, in everyday occurrences, in the most ordinary actions of life.... Revolutions, political changes, whatever occurs in general or happens to the individual, all come from God. Not even a hair of our head falls without his permission. The death of a sparrow is surely no extraordinary occurrence, yet it happens not without the will of your heavenly Father. All comes from God. To act by faith, to practice faith, and to live by faith means to consider all events, natural and supernatural, in the light in which God views them. We receive that light by faith, judge those events in that light and begin to live accordingly.[3]

Exercise

• Go back over what has happened in your life this past week. In prayer ask Jesus and Mary to reveal to you what God was saying to you in those events. (This is an excellent exercise to do whenever you make a retreat.)

EXPECTANT FAITH IN GOD'S POWER

When you drive at a steady speed along a level highway, your car stays in the same gear. But if you come to a steep hill and are driving with an automatic transmission, the car automatically shifts into a lower gear to give it more climbing power. When you need a sudden burst of speed to pass another car, you press down on the gas pedal to make it kick into higher gear.

The journey of faith is like that. For the ordinary travels, normal power suffices. But sometimes the difficult road ahead requires extra power. The expectant power of faith helps us to believe that God can change things, that he can do what is difficult (and that with his power *we* can do it). We believe that God can, in fact, do what is humanly impossible, for "nothing is impossible with God" (Lk 1:37). We pray in faith and expect God to work wonders, even miracles.

Expectant faith is the kind we see most often in the Gospels. The leper, the centurion, the blind man, the woman with the flow of blood, the Canaanite woman—all come to Jesus asking for healing. And they receive it, Jesus says, because they believe. As Fr. Chaminade said, "It was not more difficult for our Lord to raise the dead Lazarus than to cure the fever of Peter's mother-in-law. Faith contains in itself the omnipotence of God."[4]

Father Chaminade displayed this kind of faith, especially when he was convinced that certain works were inspired by God. Under his direction, Marie-Therese de Lamourous wanted to begin a home for unwed mothers. An old convent was for sale, but Miss de Lamourous had no money to buy it. She asked Fr. Chaminade what she should do.

He thought for a moment, then said, "Before answering your question, let me to ask you: Do you believe firmly that this work is the work of God?"

"Yes," she replied, "I firmly believe it."

"Do you also firmly believe that you are called to this work?"

"I firmly believe it," she said again.

"Well, then, buy not only one but both properties, the house and the church." The following year a benefactor paid off the entire debt.[5]

This kind of faith does not hesitate to ask for miracles: big miracles such as healing of terminal diseases; little miracles such as expecting God to act beyond our expectations. Under pressure to get this manuscript to the publisher, I didn't think I could make the deadline because of technical difficulties with the computer. I also faced the beginning of a new school year with classes to prepare, meetings to attend, and the phone ringing with request after request for my services and my time.

In the midst of all this pressure, I needed to straighten out a problem with a roll of film I had dropped off to be developed. When I returned the two frames which had been misprinted, the clerk made a mistake in filling out my return sheet. So one of the many phone calls came from the store telling me that I had to return to fill out another form because of the mistake the *clerk* had made.

I was infuriated. In fact, I was shocked at the intensity of my anger over what was a relatively minor problem. I hated having my time being eaten up by such a frivolous matter, a

stupid mistake. In addition to that, my community was sched-
uled to have its annual planning meeting the next day. Because
we hadn't met in quite a while, certain tensions were brewing,
and I felt anxious about the outcome.

In my distress I turned to Mary and surrendered the whole
chaos to her. I asked for a miracle: the miracle of a fruitful
meeting and the miracle of a multiplication of my time, along
with a healing of my anger. I knew Mary hadn't hesitated to
ask for a miracle at Cana and had gotten more than she asked
for. So did I. Our planning meeting was more blessed and
energizing than any I had experienced. Then the next day,
although some unexpected duties emerged to challenge my
faith, other circumstances multiplied my time in ways I hadn't
expected. Best of all, I experienced a deep peace. I'm now
learning to pray for a miracle every day, which is another way
of praying "thy kingdom come." And when I begin to look
for God's miracles in my day, he opens my eyes to see them.

We also need to apply this expectant faith of the heart to
our growth in holiness, for "this is the will of God: your sanctification" (1 Thes 4:3). Here too, we sometimes need that
"passing gear" when we encounter obstacles. Scripture warns
us that the Christian life is a combat, often with "principalities
and powers" (Col 2:15). In fighting the good fight, we need
to remember to call on the infinite power of God, which we
can tap by faith.

Exercises

- The next time someone asks you for prayers, instead of saying,
  "Yes, I will pray for you," say, "May I pray with you right
  now?" If the person is willing, pray with him or her on the
  spot—even over the phone. If you don't yet feel comfortable
  praying spontaneously, say an Our Father, Hail Mary, and
  Glory Be, asking for the favor to be granted.

- Begin by identifying a need in your spiritual life, the biggest
  need you think you have: courage, humility, honesty,

assertiveness, patience, sensitivity to others' needs, or whatever. Then, in prayer, ask Jesus to give you his strength in that area. Knowing that he will give it, see yourself acting in a new way. Evaluate your progress at the end of the day.

• Make acts of faith throughout the day, especially when in doubt or difficulty. Two powerful acts of faith are the Jesus Prayer ("Lord Jesus Christ, have mercy on me") and Sr. Faustina's prayer of Divine Mercy ("Jesus, I trust in you").

GROWING IN FAITH

One of the quickest and easiest ways to grow in faith is to unite ourselves to Mary, the woman who was praised because she believed (Lk 1:45). Mary is a model of the three kinds of faith explained above. At the annunciation, she believed and obeyed the revelation of God perfectly. Jesus said of his mother, "Blessed are those who hear the word of God and keep it" (Lk 11:28). Concerning God's care for her in the events of her life, twice St. Luke tells us, "She kept all these things, pondering them in her heart" (Lk 2:19, 51). And Mary's expectant faith at Cana won the miracle.

In practice, union with Mary means inviting her to come into our lives in a real way—into the nitty gritty of our lives, asking her to companion and to guide us at particular moments.

Faith needs to grow at every stage of our lives. Abraham, called the father of faith, provides a good example. God promised him a son, but he had to wait a long time, believing it would happen. When Abraham grew impatient and tried to do it his own way by getting a son through Hagar, the Lord said, "No, it is through Sarah, as I promised." His journey of faith didn't end there. Once his son Isaac was born, Abraham had to be willing to lose him as a test of his faith (Gn 22).

So, too, with us. Our faith is never perfectly pure. Each day as we read or listen to God's Word in faith, we receive new light and our lives are gradually changed, beginning with our hearts. When events—ordinary or extraordinary—happen, we can exercise our faith by trying to interpret them in the light of God's action in our lives. In the needs we encounter in our spiritual lives, our work, and the apostolate, we exercise our faith by turning to the true source of power and victory, the Lord.

It is above all in personal prayer that we exercise the three kinds of faith: listening to God's Word, pondering the events of our lives, and asking for what we need. When we read a passage of Scripture, we can select a word or phrase that strikes us and repeat it over and over with our lips, asking that it take over our hearts and wills. We can periodically repeat acts of faith in that word and the God who speaks it: "Lord, I believe, increase my faith." Then we can rest and let our hearts be inflamed with the reality of that word. During the day we can repeat that word often, always doing so in faith. Then in our evening prayer we can come back to it again.

At other times we can ponder what has happened in our lives today or recently, asking the Lord's light so that we can hear what he may be saying to us in those events. Finally, when confronted with needs in our lives—whether they be spiritual, emotional, physical, or intellectual—we can tap the power of Jesus in us to meet those needs. Though we exercise faith chiefly in prayer, we also put it to work through every daily action. Faith that does not act is dead. By living out our faith, we allow God to increase it in us.

All of the virtues discussed in the remainder of this book demand faith of us. In fact, each virtue is merely a facet of faith. For faith is "the beginning, the foundation, and the root of all righteousness," as the Council of Trent said. A foundation is something upon which we build. Earlier we described it as the first decision which marks the beginning of a journey. Whichever image you prefer, we are now ready to build or to travel.

In all that follows, especially when we speak of awareness,

self-knowledge, and discipline, we must always keep our eyes fixed on Jesus. In his eyes we see ourselves as infinitely loved. He assures us that even if we fall he will lift us up and help us onward. He treasures not so much the work of our becoming "perfect" as he does our trusting relationship with him.

Remember how Peter began to sink when he thought of himself and lost sight of Jesus? Even so, Jesus picked him up and gently chided him for not trusting more fully. Recalling that we are children of Mary will also help us grow in this trusting faith. Have you ever noticed how a child that falls looks first at his mother before deciding whether he should cry or not? He looks to his mother to interpret what his falling means. If his mother panics, the child will scream. If his mother smiles and reaches down gently to pick the child up, the child may whimper, but he feels he can cope with the fall. Our mother Mary doesn't panic when we fall. She's there to lift us up gently and set us on our feet again.

As we study these virtues we should not become discouraged once we discover how far we are from being perfect temples of the Holy Spirit. The system outlined in these pages is not like some mechanical thing, nor is it intended to make us scrupulous or distract us from the nourishing sunlight of God's love for us in Jesus. Rather it is meant to let that sunlight touch unhealed areas of our lives, so that like Mary we can be more and more *totus tuus*—totally yours.

Steps on the Journey

1. What does the phrase "faith of the heart" mean to you? How is this different from an intellectual faith, or faith lived only at the emotional level, or faith that does not encourage growth and maturity?

2. As you reflect on this chapter's description of the three kinds of faith, consider how in practical ways you can: (a)

listen to God's Word in Scripture, in prayer, through spiritual reading, through the events of your life, through listening to others; (b) ponder the events in your life as being signs from God which can help you to abandon those things which are not life-giving; (c) ask for whatever you need to develop an awareness of God's presence, to recognize his graces, to accept his challenges, to grow in spiritual maturity.

3. How have you experienced Mary as a help to grow in the three kinds of faith?

Lord, I do believe. Increase my faith! Teach me to cling to your Word and not to the false values of the world. Show me how to read the Father's plan in the events of my life, the painful as well as the joyful. And give me that energetic and aggressive faith that enabled the leper to say, "Lord, if you want to, you can..." Above all, let me have the faith of her who was proclaimed blessed because she believed that all the Lord had promised would be fulfilled. Amen.

Part Two

✤

Taking Hold

Taking Hold

Life is a matter of holding and letting go. A mother must hold her child in the womb long enough so that it can survive once it leaves the womb. But she must also let go of the tiny human being within her when the time for birth has come, or else both will die. Acrobats know better than anyone that "there is a time to hold on and a time to let go" (Eccl 3:5).

In the spiritual life, too, we find times for holding on and times for letting go. In this part we will look at the various ways we are challenged to take hold, to become responsible for our lives, to discipline our movements and thoughts, so that we do not fall victim to the impulse of the moment or to a herd mentality.

The price of authentic freedom is enormous. A master pianist may impress us with the spontaneity and spirit of his or her performance, but that freedom would have been impossible without years of instruction and practice to master the basics. Even after achieving stardom, most professional performers regularly spend time honing their skills. In the same way, freedom and power in the spiritual life depend in part on the discipline we've gained in the smaller, more immediate challenges of our lives.

If you are an idealist, I beg you not to despise the very simple and pragmatic areas of life which we will now explore. Awareness may sound too basic, but it provides the foundation for any growth. How do we feel about our bodies? What do we communicate physically and verbally? What does silence entail? Are we scraping by *under* the circumstances? For sanctity to be real, for mission and ministry to be well founded, attention to these practical areas of daily life is essential. Wisdom is not only a gift. It is also a way.

Imagine the great peace you would find if you walked into the house of Nazareth. You would experience a deep centeredness. You would become aware of the holiness of what Mary or Joseph or Jesus was doing at the present moment, even if it were such a prosaic thing as sweeping the floor or driving a nail. There would be a focus to their activity, suggesting that God was not a distraction from their work, nor their work from God. God's presence would be felt in their activity, not outside it. The virtues with which we begin this "way of wisdom," under the guidance of the Lady of wisdom, are the door to the holiness of Nazareth. It was a holiness that prepared Jesus for the deeply focused power of his public ministry.

SIX

Bringing Our Bodies to Jesus

PETER FOLLOWED JESUS with a full heart, but how often he had no idea of what was really going on! He may have wanted to be "all there" for Jesus, but the Gospels tell us he often fell short. Peter wasn't aware of who Jesus was; he wasn't aware that the Messiah would have to suffer; above all, he wasn't aware of his own weakness. Knowing all this, Jesus still loved Peter and tried to warn him:

> "Simon, Simon, behold Satan has demanded to sift all of you like wheat, but I have prayed that your own faith may not fail; and once you have turned back, you must strengthen your brothers."... [Peter] said to him, "Lord, I am prepared to go to prison and to die with you." But he replied, "I tell you, Peter, before the cock crows this day, you will deny three times that you know me." **Luke 22:31-34, NAB**

What can we learn from this exchange? No matter how gifted, how intelligent, how pious we may be, a tragic flaw overlooked or neglected may end up destroying our relationship with Jesus and perhaps even destroying ourselves.

Awareness comes in two kinds: awareness of what's going

on *outside* us, and awareness of what's going on *inside* us. We could call this awareness a sense of *presence*, because awareness means being actively, consciously present to the world around us, to others, and to ourselves.

An excellent exercise to put you on the road to awareness is simply to be still for ten minutes. Then become aware of your bodily sensations: sounds, smells, the feeling of the chair you're sitting on, the clothes touching your body, and so on.[1] Trying to maintain complete silence, outwardly and inwardly, for just ten minutes can be very revealing about your inner world.

Simply being aware or present marks the first step on our journey whereby we direct our energies to the Lord and to his kingdom. The first commandment, Jesus said, is to love God with our whole heart, with our whole soul, with our whole strength, and with our whole mind (Lk 10:27). But despite our ardent desire to do so, the beginning of the spiritual life often finds us more like a garden hose riddled with holes. Because so much of our energy gets poured out in a dozen different directions, only a small fraction ever reaches the mark. Patching all these holes takes time, but first we need to become aware of what kind of hose we are!

BLAMELESS BODIES

St. Paul concluded his first letter to the Thessalonians with this blessing: "May the God of peace make you holy through and through, and may your whole being, spirit, soul, and body, be kept blameless for the coming of our Lord Jesus Christ" (1 Thes 5:23).

Paul's words sound somewhat like Jesus' teaching on the first commandment to love God with our whole being. But note the differences. Jesus quotes a "command" of the old law, giving an instruction of what we should do; Paul speaks of being made holy as God's work, the effect of his grace. Jesus refers to heart, soul, strength, and mind; Paul speaks of spirit, soul, and body.

Both Jesus and Paul mean we are to grow in God's love by letting that love take over our whole being. But Paul mentions body and relates it to spirit and soul for a special reason. Many of the recent converts had been influenced by philosophies that despised the body as the prison or tomb of the soul, while others had been encouraged to indulge the body in every kind of selfish pleasure. Both sides of the issue saw the human creature as a split being. Even after their conversion to Christ, many of the gentiles had to learn that holiness involved not just the soul or spirit but also the body. Nowhere is this clearer than in 1 Corinthians 6:12-20:

[12]All things are permissible to me, but not all are helpful. All things are permissible to me, but I shall not let myself be caught under the power of anything. [13]Food is for the stomach and the stomach for food; yet God will put an end to the use of both the one and the other. The body, however, is not for fornication but for the Lord, and the Lord for the body. [14]Now just as God raised the Lord, he will raise us up too by his power. [15]Do you not realize that your bodies are members of Christ? Shall I then take the members of Christ and make them the members of a prostitute? Never! [16]Do you not realize that whoever unites himself to a prostitute becomes one body with her? So says the Scripture, "The two shall become one flesh." [17]But he who unites himself to the Lord becomes one spirit with him. [18]Flee fornication. Every other sin a man commits is outside the body, but the fornicator sins against his own body. [19]Do you not realize that your body is the temple of the Holy Spirit, who is in you, whom you have from God. You are not your own. You have been bought—and at a price! [20]So then glorify God in your body.

We can take note of several key points in this passage. Paul declares that the body, food, and sex are all good, but that we shouldn't become slaves of any of them. The body is consecrated to the Lord and his service (v. 13), destined for the glory of the resurrection (v. 14), and a member of Christ, part of his own body (v. 15). The body is the temple of the Holy Spirit (v. 19), belonging to God (v. 19), having been bought at the price of Christ's blood (v. 20). Therefore, what we do with our bodies constitutes a spiritual event (vv. 16-17). And our bodily life is to be a perpetual worship of God (v. 20).

Our Catholic faith teaches us not only that our bodies are destined to share the risen glory of Christ. It also tells us that one member of Christ has already been lifted to a share in that glory: Mary, assumed body and soul into the final glory to which the earthly church aspires. Her body was the sanctuary of the incarnation, the incredible mystery of God becoming one of us. He did so by taking on the flesh of Mary. If Mary is to lead us to Jesus, then we have to be ready to accept holiness in its earthly, human form. We have to be ready for the transformation of our bodies. There is no authentic holiness that bypasses the body.

The church's whole sacramental system is an extension of what was begun in the womb of Mary. The waters of baptism touch our bodies and we are reborn. The oil of confirmation touches our brow and we receive the anointing of the Holy Spirit. The Eucharist is the very Body and Blood of the Lord, which we take into ourselves as food.

What are the consequences of this teaching for our spiritual life? In terms of acquiring awareness and growing spiritually, there is no better place to begin than with our bodies. One simple reason is that we are most naturally aware of our physical being. A slight itch, a change in temperature, an uncomfortable chair—we feel these immediately. If the body is sacramental, as the visible, tangible sign of the spirit, then there is no better place to start.

Before engaging the body in a spiritual exercise, perhaps we should first look at our attitude toward it. Various people see the body in different ways. Consider the body-builder who

spends hours sculpting his muscles, the beautician who lav-
ishes her body with cosmetics and perfumes, the couch-potato
who neglects his body and becomes overweight, the chain-
smoker who fills her body with alcohol or drugs, the pornog-
rapher who sells seductive nudity, the Muslim woman who
remains veiled in public.

Some see the body as useful, some see it as an object of
pleasure, others as a means of power. Some delight in using
the body in sports or games or dance; others feel clumsy and
shy when they try to perform physical movements. Some trust
bodily signals; others fear these messages.

On the university campus where I teach I find signals being
constantly given by the students' body language. One weight-
lifter loves to wear a tank shirt. Guess why? Some women wear
a great deal of make-up, jewelry, and perfume; others never
wear it. Some students look sexy, others look slovenly. The
way students treat their bodies is saying a lot about how they
think of themselves. Those who have a good self-image don't
seem to feel the need to go to one extreme or the other.

How do you feel about your body? Try to reflect on your
own body image before you read further.

DO YOU LOVE YOUR BODY?

What is the Christian view of the body? Despite the severe
penances practiced by some of the saints, the Christian view
can be simply stated: God loves the body and wants us to love
it too.

To say that God loves my body is a very important part of
saying that God loves me. He doesn't just love my soul. He
made my body, and he loves what he has made. My physical
being is an expression of God's love. It doesn't take much
knowledge of biology to discover that the human body is a
miracle, a wonder. And as a Christian I believe that God has

destined my body for the risen bodily glory already enjoyed by Jesus and Mary.

God wants us to love what he loves. Yet for various reasons, many people do not love their bodies. Perhaps they feel too short, too fat, too tall, or too thin. Perhaps they focus on some embarrassing deformity or blemish which they fear will make others think less of them. And sometimes other people do hold such things against us, especially during childhood years when schoolmates can be rather merciless and cruel.

The cruelty of family or friends can be even more painful, whether intentional or not. I was born with a foot that turned in noticeably when I walked. Despite loving care and regular massage by mother and aunts, I walked pigeon-toed. This irritated my father considerably and he often scolded me for it. He seemed to think I could walk straight by sheer willpower. My childhood experience left me with a bad body image which took many years to overcome.

When I was sixteen, I became friends with a fellow who walked more pigeon-toed than I. He was a good athlete, but more importantly for me, he hardly seemed to know he was pigeon-toed. Perhaps he hadn't been reminded of the fact by his family. In any case, his slight deformity seemed to make no difference. In fact, he walked as if he enjoyed walking pigeon-toed! Gradually I began to enjoy the way I walked, too, and slowly learned to love my feet.

A well-known charismatic with an unusual gift of healing described to me one of the most dramatic healings he had ever seen. The incident happened during a conference in Colombia, South America. A sixteen-year-old girl was brought in, hobbling on a crutch. Her left leg hung limp, about ten inches shorter than her other leg, and curved inward. She had contracted a serious infection as a small child which had kept that leg from growing properly. As the prayer team began praying, the lower portion of her leg became very hot, a sign that healing was taking place.

One of the team members asked the girl, "Do you love your leg?"

"No," she said, without hesitation, "I hate it."

"Why?" asked the team member. The girl explained that her leg was an embarrassment to her parents, who had rejected her because of this deformity. Their attitude had added spiritual suffering to the girl's physical problems. The team invited her to forgive her parents, to let go of any resentment she felt toward them, and to consciously love her leg. During three hours of praying and applying love to the leg, it had grown within a half-inch of the other leg's length. (The team concluded that God had left the remaining half-inch because he wanted the parents to respond to their daughter with newfound love and acceptance. Only then would the healing be complete.)

Was not the real secret of Jesus' healing power his infinite love? If the healing of a crippled girl can happen when friends and the girl herself open up to God's love for her leg, what must it have been like when the Son of God touched the body of anyone with the immediate, infinite, life-giving love of God?

The leper, the blind man, Peter's mother-in-law, the dead daughter of Jairus—Jesus touched them all. He could have healed with a word, but he wanted them to know he accepted and loved them totally, body and soul. The woman with the twelve-year hemorrhage was very ashamed of her condition. It made her ritually unclean. She was afraid to touch Jesus lest she should defile him, so she tried a compromise by touching the hem of his garment. Jesus reassured her and healed her on the spot.

If we don't like our bodies, or if there's some part of them we don't like, then we need to open ourselves to God's love and in faith see it coming like light and heat to the part we've rejected. We may need to do this repeatedly for weeks and months. If we do we are likely to find new life flowing into us through that part. Not only that, our whole being—which may have been wounded by our rejection of a part of ourselves—will begin to be healed. (Later we will talk about loving the unloved members of Christ's body in the same way.)

DISCIPLINING THE BODY

Loving our bodies certainly doesn't mean we indulge our every whim. Parents who truly love their children don't spoil them with excess toys and treats. As children of God, disciplining our bodies in matters of diet, sleep, posture, and exercise is actually a way of loving ourselves as our heavenly Father loves us. The way we treat our bodies tells us what we really think about ourselves. Our physical discipline also reflects our spiritual health.

If we feel controlled by compulsive habits involving the body, then that is where we need to begin. Such habits can seriously oppress our freedom, even to the point of addiction. Addictions to drugs or alcohol or sexual abuse may require professional therapy in addition to prayer. Compulsions like smoking or overeating or not being able to resist certain unhealthy foods or drink (for example, the caffeine compulsion) can often be overcome by means within our power, especially prayer.[2] Addictions or compulsions not only inhibit our freedom but also our ability to be present to others.

Certain other areas of discipline, such as time management and sleep management, are extensions of our bodily life. We can take an inventory of those areas and decide to bring them under the control of the will and of the Holy Spirit. Experience has shown, however, that sheer willpower is often insufficient to overcome such negative patterns of behavior.

Addictions are particularly stubborn to uproot. The twelve steps of Alcoholics Anonymous tell us that we must begin with an admission of our powerlessness to control the addiction and our need of a power greater than ourselves to do so.

On this point, the Christian has a great resource in Jesus Christ and the power of the Holy Spirit. Surrendering our lives to Jesus gives us access to that higher power we need to set us free. A regular support group can strengthen our resolve and pick us up when we fall.

How can we pretend to be faithful Christians who are growing in the Spirit and not face these areas of inconsistency in our lives? Trying to reach the spirit without going through the body would be a grand delusion. Our God is the God of truth, as well as the God of liberation.

Whether we suffer from some bodily compulsion or not, prudent fasting is a wonderful way to school the body in the spiritual realm, as well as an excellent laboratory for awareness. Even from a purely physical point of view, occasional fasting can be beneficial for anyone in good health. But from a spiritual point of view, the hunger we choose to experience in fasting can become an external sign of our deeper hunger for God and the kingdom of God. Fasting can also increase our solidarity with the millions of people who go to bed each night with stomachs crying for food.

There are no hard and fast rules about fasting. Each person needs to discern the call to fast and to learn what he or she can and cannot do. Some find that they can fast for an entire day on liquids. Others skip a meal or fast until the evening meal. It is best not to deprive the body of liquids. Certain physical conditions, like diabetes, preclude fasting from food and suggest some other way of sacrificing. Isaiah 58 reminds us that reaching out to the oppressed and needy is the fasting that is most pleasing to God.

By learning to express yourself through your body, you are already advancing in prayer and union with God. To love and be aware of this great gift is an advance in wholeness. As St. Irenaeus said, "The glory of God is man fully alive." If you come to love your body and see it as your friend and helper, then you can begin to let it speak to you of life, of being, of God.

Exercises

- Take a comfortable position and determine that you will sit perfectly still for fifteen minutes. Even if part of your body begins to itch or ache, do not move. It will help to begin with an act of faith in the presence of God, but don't worry about thinking anything. Just be perfectly still for the entire time. You will probably notice this has a calming effect on your mind, your emotions, and your whole inner being.

- "To you I lift up my hands...." Follow the above stillness exercise by looking at your hands for a few minutes. Don't analyze; just look. See the wonder of your hands. Feel the gift they are. What would you do without them? Reflect on all the things you can do with your hands—work, write, touch others, greet people, and hug them. Then gently turn your palms upward and again look at them for a while. Consider the wonder of these hands, these fingers.

  Now slowly and prayerfully move your hands outward and hold them there in a position of giving and receiving. Let them speak to the Lord for you—your desire to receive God's gifts and to give yourself wholly to him.

  Then gradually lift your arms to a higher position and let them continue to express the same receiving-giving attitude. Keep them in this position for a while even after you begin to feel a little discomfort. Now lift your arms to their full length upward and outward, and let them speak your most intense desire to receive from the Lord and to give yourself to him.

- Do the same exercise while kneeling. After kneeling a while, prostrate yourself completely, face down, before the tabernacle, crucifix, or an image of the Lord. Let your body speak for you.

- Using a compact disc, record, or tape of sacred music or song, act out the music or song with gestures, movement, or dance—as the Spirit leads you. You might prefer to do this exercise when you're alone, but it can also be done in a group. Everyone can "do their own thing" at first, and then create a dance together to the same song.[3]

Steps on the Journey

1. What is your attitude toward your body? Do you accept it as God's gift? Do you appreciate it as destined to share the bodily glory of Jesus and Mary? Do you feel bad about any part of it? Do you love your body as God does?

2. How do you express prayer through your body? Does your bodily posture express reverence or a careless attitude toward the presence of God? Do the bodily movements used in the liturgy mean anything to you—bowing, kneeling, sitting, standing, offering the greeting of peace to your brothers and sisters?

3. Do you care properly and without anxiety for your health? Does your diet primarily consist of good food or junk food? Do you get proper exercise? Do you retire early enough so as to be alert the next day? Could you improve the discipline of your body?

4. What compulsions or addictions inhibit your freedom? How will you respond to the Lord's call to freedom?

Lord Jesus, you took our flesh in the womb of Mary, that you might redeem our bodies as well as our souls and that you might teach us how to belong totally to God, body and soul. You have promised us that if we are faithful to you we will share with you and with your mother bodily glory in the resurrection. Help me to love and to discipline my body that it may reach the full perfection to which you call me. Amen.

SEVEN

The Body as a Bridge

S CRIPTURE SPEAKS of the body not as a prison of the soul, nor as a barrier isolating us from others, but as a *bridge*. The body tells us of our relationships, to God, to others, and to creation as a whole. As a gateway to the spirit, the body is a means of achieving inward awareness, moving toward deeper union with God. But our physical being also serves as a communicator to others.

Our radical relationship is with the earth. The name Adam comes from *adamah*, meaning earth. And my name too is Adam because I am Earthman. I am therefore brother or sister to every created thing, the earth, the sky, every tree and flower. St. Francis realized this profound truth when he sang of Brother Sun and Sister Moon.

We are elder brothers or sisters of the universe in the sense that we are responsible for it. We must care for creation and use it for the glory of God. His original plan included peace between humankind and all of creation (as we see in the Garden of Eden).

So why doesn't the human race experience this peace? Because our wounded and sinful condition makes our relationship to creation painful and toilsome. After the fall, God told Adam and Eve, "Thorns and thistles shall the earth bring forth for you... and you shall eat bread by the sweat of your brow" (Gn 3:18-19).

Christians, however, embrace a profound hope because Jesus has risen from the dead. We believe that all creation will be renewed when our bodies are glorified. Because our bodies are joined to the earth and all material creation, when they are made glorious, they will bring something of the whole created order into the new world (see Rom 8:18-23; Eph 1:21-23; Phil 3:21).

COMMUNION WITH THE EARTH

What consequences does this relationship between our bodies and all of creation have for our spiritual life? First, we need to keep in touch with the earth. If we want to have a conscious awareness of who we are as earth people, we need to take time to get in touch with what we sense and what we feel.

People whose occupations bring them into contact with the earth and its physical components ordinarily come by this awareness naturally. Those engaged in administrative or intellectual work often find that manual labor like gardening or yard work helps them to get more in touch with their own bodiliness and their solidarity with the earth. We might call this "physical humility," since the word "humility" comes from the Latin word *humus*, meaning soil.

The first Christian hermits who lived in the desert quickly discovered this link between work and humility, something which became an important element of monastic life thereafter. For St. Benedict, the monk's life was summed up in the Latin words *ora et labora*—pray and work.

Work that puts us in direct contact with matter is therapeutic, a principle applied by therapists who use manual work and crafts in the treatment of mental patients. During my stay in Switzerland, I had studied intensely for months in preparation for a comprehensive exam in theology. The day after I passed the exam, I was on a train to Vienna to study German in preparation for my doctoral work. After about ten days of beating my head against the books, I was experiencing fatigue and depression. I volunteered to help wash windows the next day, and by that evening felt completely restored, with energy to spare.

Other experiences can accomplish the same purpose. For example, try walking barefoot outside and consciously feel the blades of grass. Instead of swallowing your food in haste, take time to savor it, chewing and enjoying each bite (an aid to digestion as well). Let your eyes drink in the beauty of nature. Let yourself gently and peacefully enjoy the smell of a flower, as a child would. Don't bother about putting a name or a label on the flower. Don't work at bringing God into the picture from the outside. Just let the flower lead you into the joy of existence and of knowing God.

Exercises

- Take off your shoes and socks and walk on the grass. Center your being on feeling the grass, forgetting everything else. The experience can be a prayer. Let your spirit and heart respond as you are led.

- Hold a flower in your hand. Look at it and let it look back at you. Do this for a period of at least ten minutes. Just enjoy it, don't analyze. Listen to see if the flower speaks to you. What does it say? Be aware of any thoughts that come gently. If you're in a group, share your experience with one another. Then read Isaiah 43:1-5, noting especially: "You are precious in my eyes and I love you." Now return to the flower exercise and allow yourself to delight in the flower. Imagine that the flower is you and reflect that the Father delights in you infinitely more than you do in the flower. (Jesus said, "Consider the lilies...")

- Do an exercise similar to the flower one with any other bit of creation (a leaf or a plant, for example).

REACH OUT AND TOUCH SOMEONE

As a bridge, our bodies relate us not only to the earth and to the universe but also to others. When Paul needed an image to explain our mysterious unity in Christ, he could find no better one than the body: "Now you are the body of Christ, and each one is a part of it" (1 Cor 12:27).

For Paul being members of one body held enormous practical ramifications. It means to rejoice with those who rejoice and to mourn with those who mourn. We are to "remember those who are in prison, as though in prison with them; and those who are ill-treated, since you are also in the body" (Heb 13:3). "Put away all lying, then! We must tell the truth to one another, because we are all members together in the body of Christ" (Eph 4:25).

Scripture presents the body as a bridge, a way of reaching others, a means of union and brotherhood. In fulfilling these purposes, we must use our bodies for communication. Let's consider how body language can help us to come closer to God and to others.

The Bible recounts many occasions on which Jesus communicated powerfully without words. For example, he healed the leper with a touch (Mt 8:1-3). This action takes on special meaning when we remember that the leper was an outcast; Jesus contracted ritual defilement by touching him. He took Peter's mother-in-law by the hand and lifted her up (Mt 8:14-15). He did the same with Jairus' daughter (Mt 9:25). Immediately after Peter denied his Master three times, one look from Jesus was sufficient to dissolve a burly fisherman into tears (Lk 22:61-62).

When the Pharisees presented the woman taken in adultery, the Lord showed his disinterest in their accusations by saying nothing and writing on the ground instead (Jn 8:6-8). Zacchaeus wanted to see Jesus. To his surprise, Jesus looked up at this short tax collector perched on the limb of a tree (Lk 19:4-

5). Jesus looked with love at the young man who had kept all the commandments (Mk 10:21). And at the Last Supper, before explaining what he was doing, Jesus got up from the table, girded himself with a towel, and began washing the feet of his disciples (Jn 13:1-5).

Jesus said that his disciples were to be the light of the world and the salt of the earth (Mt 5:13-16). Fulfilling these words means far more than preaching. The world should be able to see the light of God in the way believers live. If a picture is worth a thousand words, certainly a gesture, an action, a movement can often convey much more than words. I remember holding the hand of my father, and later of my mother, as they were dying. And I remember holding the hand of a dying brother. That simple gesture communicated more than my words.

The range of body language includes gestures, gait, posture, looks, eating habits, manners, care of our bodies, physical appearance, and dress. Our living environment is also a form of nonverbal communication. Our body language can convey the good news of Jesus Christ. Unfortunately, it can also convey more subtly and often more powerfully than words our negative reactions to individuals. We can hurt others, whether they're present or not, by expressions of disdain, contempt, indifference, and boredom.

A professor or a homilist may be the only person speaking, but each member of the class or congregation is communicating by their actions: reading extraneous material, yawning, gazing elsewhere, or focusing attentively on the speaker. Whenever I give a homily, how welcome it is to see in the congregation a nod of agreement rather than one of sleep!

Speakers can communicate by maintaining eye contact, an effective way of "being present" to the audience. While most people don't like to be stared at, everyone appreciates speakers who convey their message by looking directly at the person being addressed. If the speaker seems too shy or lost in notes, the listener may wonder, *What's wrong with me? What makes the speaker afraid to look at me?*

I had a seminary professor who was an eminent Scripture scholar. He always read from his notes. Aware that he should occasionally come up for air, this professor would look up. But he always looked out the window, never at anyone in the class!

After studying this virtue of body language, a parishioner said, "But that's our problem in this parish. We don't show people a warm welcome here!" She understood that a welcoming smile, a handshake, or a gesture of friendship would be exactly what Jesus and Mary would do!

Mary's recorded words in the Bible are few. But her presence is noted particularly by John, first at the wedding feast of Cana: "And the mother of Jesus was there" (Jn 2:1). Then at Calvary she says nothing, but her presence speaks volumes as she endures in her facial expressions and in her heart all that Jesus is suffering on the cross. Then she cradles her Son's body in her arms, beautifully captured for all ages in Michelangelo's *Pieta*. In some of the reported Marian apparitions Mary says nothing. Her bodily appearance and her compassionate motherly face are sufficient. In many of life's situations all that is called for is our presence. Ogden Nash once put it very laconically: "Ninety percent of life is just showing up."

How do we become aware of our body language? Personal reflection may help, but often we're unaware of how our expressions or mannerisms affect others until someone tells us. An honest and courageous friend is irreplaceable. May we have the humility to ask for feedback and to listen!

Exercises

- Use any Gospel scene and contemplate Jesus' body language. Where the text doesn't give any clues, let your imagination recreate the scene. Then imagine how Jesus might communicate with his body in a typical scene from your own life.

- Choose one of the mysteries of the rosary and contemplate Mary's body language: her warm welcome, her joy, her compassion, her reaching out to others, her cradling of the baby Jesus. Invite Mary into your own life in similar scenes. Ask the grace to imitate her not only in inner faith but in outward expression.

Steps on the Journey

1. What do your facial expressions and bodily postures convey, especially when you should be present to others? Does your body language express openness or disinterest?

2. Do you fear eye contact with other people? If so, why?

3. What do you think Mary conveyed to others by her eye contact, her gestures, and her bodily stance?

Lord Jesus, I thank you that you have made me a member of your mystical body. I thank you that you have called me to be the light of the world. Help me to realize more deeply that what I communicate to others by my body language is often more important than what I say or don't say. Your gaze touched people deeply. The touch of your hand healed. Your mother spoke mostly by her loving presence. Take me, body and soul, and make me an instrument of life and love for others. Amen.

EIGHT

The Power of the Tongue

I DON'T REMEMBER saying my first word. Nor do I remember my parents' delight when I said it. But it wasn't long before I got the message that growing up and measuring up to their expectations meant that I had to learn words and put them together to make sentences. Formal education extended those expectations to writing paragraphs, then short essays, and finally term papers. Graduate school presented another awful hurdle: the thesis. Now here I am writing books!

Communication skills are highly prized in our culture. We are often judged by whether we can communicate correctly, and praised if we can communicate beautifully. The Bible is not so concerned with correct or beautiful speech as it is with *righteous* speech. After body language, verbal communication is the most obvious way we reveal ourselves to others.

Words of love or hate are especially potent instruments in building up or destroying Christ's body. When Jesus spoke, the crowds "were amazed at the gracious words that fell from his lips" (Lk 4:22). Grace-filled words build life in others and in the community. "Use only helpful words, the kind that build up as the occasion calls for, so that what you say will be an occasion of grace for those who hear you" (Eph 4:29).

WORDS CAN CREATE OR DESTROY

The Old Testament speaks of the power of the word. God creates by his Word, and so do human beings. "By the word of the Lord the heavens were made; by the breath of his mouth all their host" (Ps 33:6; cf. 147:15-18). God's Word spoken through the prophets foretold the future of his people: "For just as from the heavens /the rain and snow come down /And do not return there /till they have watered the earth, /making it fertile and fruitful, /Giving seed to him who sows and bread to him who eats, /So shall my word be /that goes forth from my mouth; /It shall not return to me void, /but shall do my will, /achieving the end for which I sent it" (Is 55:10-11, NAB).

Human words as well have the power to create or destroy. A father's blessing went forth from his mouth and created his son's future. Once given, it could not be withdrawn, as we see in the story of Isaac's blessing (by mistake) of Jacob (Gn 27:1-45). After giving his word of blessing to the wrong son, Isaac could not even consider retracting it. Isaac could only give Esau a secondary blessing to balance the one given to Jacob.

While Scripture extols righteous speech, no acts are more often condemned than the sins of the tongue. "By your words you will be justified, and by your words you will be condemned" (Mt 12:37). The tongue is like a flame that can set a forest afire (Jas 3:5-6). Words can hurt worse than the blows of a fist: "A blow from a whip raises a welt, /but a blow from the tongue smashes bones. /Many have fallen by the edge of the sword, /but not as many as by the tongue" (Sir 28:17-18, NAB). The Book of Sirach has lengthy and perceptive warnings about evil speech (Sir 5:12-6:1; 19:5-16; 20:17-25; 23:7-15; 28:12-26).

Few people are really aware of the power of their words for good or evil! The tongue can build up; the tongue can destroy. James likens this member of our bodies to the rudder of a ship. Those who discipline their speech reach an awareness of their inner selves and achieve the first step in self-control:

> We all fall short in many respects. If anyone does not fall short in speech, he is a perfect man, able to bridle his whole body also. If we put bits into the mouths of horses to make them obey us, we also guide their whole bodies. It is the same with ships: even though they are so large and driven by fierce winds, they are steered by a very small rudder wherever the pilot's inclination wishes. In the same way the tongue is a small member and yet has great pretensions.
>
> James 3:1-5, NAB

How do we become more aware of our habits of speech? First, determine whether you are the kind of person who talks a lot, or one who talks little. The extrovert, we are told, talks in order to think. The introvert, on the other hand, thinks in order to talk. While neither tendency is virtuous or evil of itself, knowing our inclinations will help us to understand and accept ourselves and others. If we tend to be talkative, we could work on keeping a more sensitive silence and listening better. If we tend to be shy, we may need to become more assertive, to speak up, to express our thoughts and feelings more readily.

Scripture tells us that there is "a time to be silent, and a time to speak" (Eccl 3:7). The most important fruit of being attentive to our speech and our silence is an increased awareness of ourselves before God. Daily journaling can be helpful. After a period of time, we can look back over our entries and see what we have learned about ourselves.

A UNIVERSAL LANGUAGE

We see the "breakdown of communication" in families that bicker, in groups that are contentious, and in nations that eventually go to war. The first eleven chapters of Genesis detail how sin so ruptured the social landscape that people could no longer communicate with each other. The tower of Babel was built to reach into the heavens and glorify human achievement, but became instead a maze of walls keeping the people apart.

The Holy Spirit came on Pentecost to reverse the curse of divisive communication. The divine electricity "jumped" the space between nations and languages, between slave and free, between rich and poor, showing that no human differences need stand in the way of God's love. The tongues of Pentecost, like music, were a universal language.

Since so much of our lives revolves around communication, why not make a virtue of it? But communicating in a holy way every day is not easy. Do we gossip about the faults of others? Are we short on compliments and long on criticisms? Do we gripe about a situation but do nothing about it? Do we talk *about* others rather than *to* them (especially when they do something we don't like)? Do we do most of the talking? Do we interrupt others before hearing them out? If so, why do we consider what we have to say more important than listening to what others have to say?

Virtuous communication is largely a matter of learning how to listen. Often people respond (especially in the midst of a disagreement) before the other person has a chance to fully explain his or her position. We can be sure we understand people only when we can correctly repeat to them what we think they have said. Many an argument could be avoided by this simple procedure.

More importantly, we should listen to what is coming from the person's heart. When we understand "where the person is coming from," we can respond in a more constructive way. That doesn't mean we will always agree with the person, but it means that we can disagree without being disagreeable. As Pope John XXIII is reported to have said, "I will walk together with anyone as far as I can, until truth and charity require me to go a separate way." (In a later section, "Silence of the Heart," we will examine the specific communication problem that results from our negative feelings about others.)

Often the virtue of communication demands silence. The ascetics of the desert learned long ago the value of silence. Monks and nuns practiced it for centuries in the monasteries. We often need to be silent to experience the presence of God: "Be still and know that I am God" (Ps 46:11). This isn't the dead silence of a corpse, or the deadly silence of people refusing to communicate with each other. It is rather the creative silence which allows being, reality, and God himself to speak to us. Individuals incapable of such silence tend to be superficial.

We live in a culture of noise: blaring radios, the omnipresent TV, traffic, walkmans, and CDs all claim our attention. At times we wonder if we ever belong to ourselves, or if we merely live out a script written by the sounds that daily flood our consciousness. Silence offers us a chance to take control, if even for a short time, of the outer world that wants to become our inner world.

Mary's words in the Gospels are few. Perhaps the lesson here is that she listened deeply before speaking. At the annunciation she asked how as a virgin she could become a mother. And when she was told how it would happen, she simply said, "I am the servant of the Lord. Let it be done to me as you say" (Lk 1:38). The call she was given was the awesome one of becoming the mother of God. Any ordinary woman would probably have been so overwhelmed as to forget anything else the angel said. But Mary heard the whole message, including the part about Elizabeth's pregnancy, which Mary immediately interpreted as a need to which she must attend.

At Cana her keen eye noticed the failing wine, and all she said to Jesus was, "They have no wine." She did not nag. And all she said to the waiters was, "Do whatever he tells you."

Her listening is extolled three times in Luke's Gospel, twice when we are told she kept all these things, pondering them in her heart, and once when Jesus said, "Blessed are they who hear the word of God and keep it." She listened not only to the Word of God as it came to her through the angel, but also to the events through which God spoke in her life, especially in the needs of others. And on Calvary her silent presence was all that Jesus needed. What a beautiful balance of listening and speaking we find in Mary!

Meditations

Meditate on the following Scriptures: Sirach 5:12-6:1; 19:5-16; 20:4-7, 17-25; 23:7-15; 28:12-26; Proverbs 10:19; 13:3; 14:23; 18:13; Psalm 141:3; Matthew 12:36-37; Luke 2:19; James 1:19, 26; 3:1-12; Ephesians 4:25-31; 5:4; 1 Peter 4:10.

Exercises

- Choose any of the mysteries of the rosary in which Mary is involved and reflect on both her words and her silence. Consider what it means that she "kept all these things, pondering them in her heart."

- Reflect on one of the Scripture passages quoted above and evaluate your own communication habits.

❦

Steps on the Journey

1. Do your words hurt or heal? What situations cause you to abuse the power of speech?

2. Do you speak too little (so that people wonder if you're involved in the conversation), or too much (dominating the conversation)? Do you try to converse with someone who has been overlooked?

3. What do you talk about most? What kind of jokes do you habitually tell?

4. What does the image of Mary suggest to you about creative listening? Are you a good listener? How have you grown in this area?

5. What about these danger signs: speaking too rapidly, too softly, too loudly, interrupting others, using profanity, putting down others through negative humor, making fun of them?

Lord Jesus, I want to follow you. I want to imitate you. I want your Holy Spirit to inspire and rule my life. But much of the way I speak and act shows how far I am from reflecting your love, your peace, your use of words to build the kingdom. Lord, open my lips not only to proclaim your praise but also to convey blessing and goodness to others. And set a guard over my mouth, lest I sin with my lips. Mary, show me the fruitfulness of your silence and the measured power of your words. Amen.

NINE

Order in the Control Room: Transforming the Past

TOM'S LIFE WAS IN JEOPARDY two years ago; now he's alive and well because someone else's heart became his own. Stephanie thrives because three years ago surgeons replaced her failing kidney with a healthy one. This miracle of modern medicine is called the transplanting of bodily organs.

Can you imagine what it would be like to live just one day with the mind and memory and imagination and heart of Jesus replacing your own—in such a way that those faculties would be truly yours? You would think his thoughts, live by his memories, be moved by his images, and feel as he feels. What a revolutionary experience!

Impossible? Medically and physically, yes. Spiritually, no. Instead of transplantation, this spiritual operation is called *transformation*. By our baptism, the seeds of Christ's life were planted in us. Through the action of the Holy Spirit, the leading of Mary, and our own faith-filled cooperation, a gradual transformation takes place deep within that enables us to act more like Jesus outwardly and think and feel more like Jesus inwardly.

Taking on the mind and heart of Jesus is a tall order, one

which would remain just an inspiring ideal if we had no practical way of cooperating with the marvelous action of the Holy Spirit. Rather than squirming under the divine surgeon's knife, how can we participate in this spiritual transformation?

When I was ten years old I had to have my tonsils removed. I was frightened at the prospect of losing my consciousness to the anesthetic and of what the surgeon would do to me. But my mother, a registered nurse who had assisted many an operation before, was at my bedside with her touch, her smile. She was my assurance not only that I needed the operation, but that I could come through it successfully and be happier and healthier on the other side. Jesus has given us his mother as the same kind of comforting presence as we go through spiritual surgery.

INNER SILENCE

As we saw in the last three chapters, spiritual growth begins with becoming aware of the body and its outward expressions of words and gestures. But that is only the first step toward awareness and silence on a more important level: the inner life.

If the Holy Spirit is to take control of that level, then we must become aware of how the inner life functions. We begin by discerning what is already going on inside of us. Is a particular activity inspired by the Holy Spirit, by the world, by an evil spirit, or by our own selfishness? While the inner life is the more significant realm to bring under God's reign, it is often the most difficult to recognize, to accept, and to turn over to the Lord.

Our Mother Mary can help us move honestly and gently into this unknown land and show us, step by step, how to let it become the domain of the Lord Jesus.

Try an initial exercise of inner awareness. Close your eyes, keep your body perfectly still, and just "blank out" the thoughts that cross your mind. You will probably find dozens of distractions moving across your mental screen. Where do they come from? Ordinarily these distractions fall into three categories:

1. *Memories of recent events in your life.* (Any vivid memories from the distant past are very important; take note of them for future reference.)

2. *Thoughts or images concerning the range of possibilities in the immediate future.* Will you pass the test? How can you get all your work done today? How can you resolve a serious relationship difficulty? Will you have enough money to pay the bills this month?

3. *Thoughts concerning your immediate sensory information* (a delivery truck passing outside your window, someone's radio blaring in the next room, co-workers conversing near your desk, an ambulance siren wailing in the distance).

Thus, our inner attention is inclined to go in one of three directions: the *past* (what has been); the *future* (what will or could be); and the *present* (what is). Three different faculties come into play in this process: *memory* directs our attention to the past; *imagination* suggests possibilities for the future; and the *mind* sorts through information concerning the present.

These faculties are a rich source of life for us. But they can also have a debilitating influence on us, sapping our mental and spiritual health. We need to ask a key question: "Who is in charge here?" Are we in charge, or are frequent distractions in charge of our lives? Are we ruled by certain memories, or fantasies, or preoccupations? Or do we have enough inner awareness and control to be able to say we are in charge? Are we master or slave?

Most of us would have to admit that we are a mixture of both master and slave. For example, we may decide at the beginning of the day that we want to move in a certain direction. We may first plan to pray and then accomplish a certain task. We usually begin well enough, but soon find ourselves being pulled off the path by such things as a distracting memory or fantasy; and inevitably there is an emotional content to these distractions. Before we realize what has happened, our original intentions seem like ancient history.

We cannot give to God what we do not possess. The first step in trying to give ourselves to the Lord, to Mary and her mission, is to gain possession of ourselves. And the first step to self-possession is awareness of what is really going on in the inner life.

This has been called the work of attaining *inner silence.* Just as verbal silence doesn't mean the absence of speech, so inner silence doesn't mean the absence of activity. It means rather awareness and direction of activity.

We will now examine each of these faculties in turn: memory, imagination, mind, and heart. We need not cover all of them at once. In fact, each one could require a month's work or more. In the rest of this chapter we will look at the role of our memory.

MEMORY: A PERSONAL HISTORY BOOK

Perhaps more than any other faculty, our memories give us a sense of identity. Those who return to consciousness after a serious accident but cannot remember anything will also not be able to identify themselves. The philosopher Martin Heidegger said, "A man is what he is—and his history." Your history has made you who you are today, but if you lose all sense of your history—your memory—you will also lose your sense of identity. You might as well start life over again since the very foundation of your self-understanding has been swept away.

Memory is crucial not only for the identity of the individual but also for the identity of a group, a community, a people. This is why the Bible insists on telling and retelling the story of God's people—such as Abraham, Moses and the Exodus, the time in the desert, the promised land, the stories of the kings and the prophets, the exile and the return.

The church continues to enliven our collective memory in a number of ways. Because Jesus said, "Do this in memory of me," we celebrate the Eucharist as a memorial sacrifice. Each year the church reenacts the Old Testament period of hope during Advent, the birth of Jesus at Christmas, the passion, death, and resurrection of Jesus through Lent and Easter, and the coming of the Holy Spirit at Pentecost. We celebrate yearly festivals at which important stories can be retold and dramatized here and now.

In fact, the Bible considers forgetfulness of God's blessings to be serious folly:

> Bless the Lord, O my soul;
>> and all my being, bless his holy name.
> Bless the Lord, O my soul,
>> and forget not all his benefits.
> He pardons all your iniquities,
>> he heals all your ills.
> He redeems your life from destruction,
>> he crowns you with kindness and compassion.
> He fills your lifetime with good;
>> your youth is renewed like the eagle's.
>
> **Psalm 103:1-5, NAB; emphasis mine**

Luke presents Mary as a model of this kind of holy remembering. Twice he tells us Mary kept all the events she was experiencing, pondering them in her heart (Lk 2:19, 51). We can assume that this was something she did during her entire life. The Greek word for "pondering" means more than remembering. It means comparing what she was experiencing with other events in the past, particularly the events in the sacred history of her people, for God seemed to be doing again in her life what he had done with Abraham and Sarah, with Manoah and his wife announcing the birth of Samson, with David and his descendants. She can teach us to find in the Scriptures a mirror of our own walk with the Lord.

Jesus tells us that the Holy Spirit is given to us to bring back to our memory all that he said and did: "The Paraclete, the Holy Spirit whom the Father will send in my name, will instruct you in everything, and remind you of all that I told you" (Jn 14:26).

Yet each of us has a unique history and a personal memory of that history. Just as the history of God's people reveals God himself to those with eyes of faith, so our personal history can be for us a true revelation of God—*if* we can learn to use our memory in the service of our faith.

The storehouse of our memory contains countless blessings we have received. We may have rarely brought them to mind but they are there: the gift of life itself, our birth, our parents, our birthplace, our families, the Christian community, our teachers, our education—and so on.

Reviewing our lives and consciously recalling our blessings enables us to experience humble gratitude and to praise God for all our blessings.

Exercise

- Take an hour of quiet time for prayer. After placing yourself in God's presence, review your life from your earliest memory until now. Try to count all the blessings of your life and realize that each one is an unmerited gift of your heavenly Father. Experience his love and thank him for all his gifts. (If sad or painful memories appear, jot them down for future reference in a later exercise, but do not dwell on them in this exercise.)

PAINFUL MEMORIES

As we prayerfully review our past, some memories may stir up disturbance and pain rather than joy and praise. We may remember physical hurts received in an accident or illness, or beatings endured deservedly or undeservedly from parents, teachers, playmates, or others. Or we may harbor emotional or spiritual hurts, perhaps times when we were rejected or betrayed or abused by someone. If that person was a parent or relative, or someone whose love we felt we deserved, the memory may be extremely painful.

Some memories are so traumatic that we repress them. This kind of incident doesn't just drop out of our memory like so many other things that we didn't consider important at the time. We usually bury it because we can't stand the pain at the time. We just pretend it didn't happen, or at least we determine never to think about it again. But a repressed memory never really dies. It lies deep in the subconscious where it continues to be active.

One young man had a terrible fear of water. Even after he learned to swim, he never wanted to go near a river. Afraid that he might fall into the water, this man almost panicked when he had to cross a footbridge. Where did his fear come from? When he was a child, his father thought he would teach his son to swim by tying a rope around him and throwing him into the river. The father expected that the boy would learn to swim out of necessity. That memory—which the boy had repressed because he couldn't admit to himself his father could be so cruel—was the cause of his later fears. The memory was repressed, but it was still active!

A woman attending a weekend retreat asked me if I could help her overcome her fear of trusting others. Since we didn't have time for lengthy counseling, I asked her to pray with me for a few moments. As we prayed, the image of a wooden fence with a green pasture beyond it came to my mind. "Does this scene mean anything to you?"

"Yes," the woman answered. "When I was three years old I was on my grandfather's farm. There was a fence and a pasture like that. A horse was on the other side of the fence. I gathered a handful of grass and offered it to him. He bit me.

Could that be where my problem of trust started?"

In severe cases, exploring repressed memories is work for a professional psychiatrist or psychologist. In ordinary situations, prayer and reflection on one's past, perhaps with the help of a spiritual director or a competent prayer team, are often sufficient to discover memories that dampen our spiritual freedom.

A FORETASTE OF HELL

One of the ways painful memories continue to act on us is through resentment or bitterness. Our hearts become a clenched fist against the person who hurt us. Of course we ourselves suffer the most from that resentment. Anyone who cannot forgive experiences a foretaste of hell, where no one asks forgiveness and no one gives it.

Forgiveness is thus the key to the healing of hurts. Other people may not be aware they've hurt us and thus not ask our forgiveness. To forgive doesn't mean we approve or condone an evil or hurtful act. It simply means that we forgive. We leave our forgiveness at the other's doorstep, ready to be picked up whenever he or she chooses to open the door and take it.

Other kinds of memories may block our present freedom, such as those that stir up feelings of guilt. Guilt in itself is not necessarily bad. If we feel guilty about doing something wrong, we should thank God for an operative conscience. God has given us a simple way to handle that guilt: confess our sin and repair the damage as best we can.

Some guilt feelings, however, are not healthy. We may feel guilty about something for which we weren't responsible. For example, let's say I was involved in an accident in which another person was killed, and yet there was nothing I could have done to prevent it. If I continue to feel guilty about it for weeks and months and years, then that memory is keeping me imprisoned. That kind of guilt is not healthy.

Or let's say I did something wrong and repented of it, confessed it, and accepted God's forgiveness—yet still feel a burden of guilt. Then I haven't forgiven myself, even though God has forgiven me. Hidden pride often says, "I really never should have done that," which may also mean, "I'm too nice a person to do that—I could never have done that." I may still be punishing myself with the thought that I, a perfect person, did the impossible, committed a sin! In that case, I need to ask God to help me experience the full joy of the forgiveness he has already extended.

Memories of sexual situations or encounters may return at moments of weakness and invite us to re-experience something we once left behind or repented of. We need to see these memories as temptations which can be met by prayer and other spiritual strategies.

Women who have had an abortion often repress the fact, sometimes for years. But eventually they will have to deal with it. Even after a good confession, some women are tormented with guilt. Some experience nightmares. This is a particularly traumatic memory that may call for post-abortion counseling and prayer, such as is provided by the Rachel movement.

In summary, we can use our blessings to glorify God and our painful memories to invite healing which leads to more praise of him and more spiritual freedom for us. Doing so allows the sanctification of one important faculty of our inner selves. If our memory becomes holy, then we also become holier. We then become more free to be present to God, ourselves, and others!

We begin to experience the kind of integration of past and present which we see in Mary. She had no personal or false guilt to deal with, but she did have painful memories which we call "the sorrowful mysteries" of her life. Yet she allowed the Holy Spirit to teach her that "for those who love God, he makes all things work together unto good" (Rom 8:28), and even in this life she saw a glimpse of the glory that lay beyond the cross. Let her, who stood beneath the cross, stand at your side, as you bring to the surface the hidden crosses of your life, and you will more quickly find your wounds transformed, like those of Jesus, into badges of victory.

Exercises

- A healing of memories service can be done in private prayer, but is usually more effective when done in a group. With gentle background music, the leader guides the group in a review of life from conception, throughout the stages of childhood, adolescence, and adulthood up to the present moment, with appropriate pauses. The leader instructs everyone to invite Jesus and Mary to enter each event or stage with their healing presence.

- Getting in touch with our memory could lead to the writing of one's spiritual autobiography, in the tradition of St. Augustine's *Confessions* or Thomas Merton's *Seven Storey Mountain*. If you are so inclined, it might be best to begin by sketching a symbolic scene from each period of your life, and then writing your memories of that period, letting the sketch serve as an illustration. More than just story-telling, this recounting should be in praise of God for the blessings of each period. If you wish, your story could also share painful memories that have been healed by God's grace, or a frank expression of questions that remain.

Steps on the Journey

1. What are some of the happiest memories of your life? Do you see them as gifts? Do you occasionally review them and praise and thank God for them?

2. Have you repressed any painful memories? Can you now allow those memories to surface and bring them to the

healing power of Jesus (in personal prayer or in a group of trusted friends who will listen, support, and pray with you)?

3. How does the thought of Mary walking with you through your memories (the happy and the painful) help you transform them?

Father, I thank you for the years of life you have given me, and for the rich store of memories they offer me. In Jesus I know all these memories can be transformed into praise, even the very painful ones. Mary, show me how to turn my happy memories into magnificats. And be at my side when painful memories surface with the assurance that they too can become sources of light and life to myself and to others. Amen.

Order in the Control Room: Transforming the Future

IMAGINATION: CREATIVE TRICKSTER

R ECALL A RECENT DREAM you had. Did it include familiar images of people or places or things? What seemed to be unfamiliar? Dreams usually cast someone close to us in unexpected situations. For example, you might see your mother falling out of a tree, something you never remember happening in her lifetime.

A dream is a magnificent exercise of our imagination, unrestrained by any rational control, somewhat like a novel or play acted out by our subconscious mind. Especially vivid dreams can have a lasting effect on our mood. We may wake up sweating from fear, or else laughing at the hilarious scenes.

Dreams demonstrate the tremendous creative power of our imagination. Artists, dancers, and novelists are especially gifted with imagination. Without their fertile imagination we would have no paintings, no new dances, no entertaining stories. Scientists use imagination to make new discoveries, to proceed on hunches that may lead to discovering a new star or a new medicine. Imagination helps break the boredom of life by offering a new way of looking at old things. And in prayer it enables us to re-live the stories of Jesus and Mary or the mysteries of the rosary, to enter into them as we would into a play, and then to let them change our lives.

Like the memory, our imagination can also trick and deceive us. Exaggeration and embellishment make use of imagination, especially through communication and humor. For example, political cartoons exaggerate notable features so that the reader will immediately recognize the subject. But exaggeration can also be an outright lie, and lying is the predominant sin of the imagination.

Suppose someone makes a slightly negative remark to me. My imagination can take this little remark and blow it up like a balloon: "That person really hates me. What did I do to deserve that? I must really be a bad person if what he says is true!" I feel depressed and moody for the rest of the day. Or the person for whom I left a phone message didn't return my call. I begin to imagine all kinds of motives behind the lack of response, such as rejection or disinterest.

The unbridled imagination loves to cast us in the role of the hero, either the "suffering hero" or the "conquering hero." Hypochondriacs who always imagine they're sick may moan and groan under their imagined suffering. They are very unlike the eighty-one-year-old rancher I once asked, "What do you do when you begin to feel aches or pains?"

"I just keep moving," he said. "Can't waste time dwelling on it."

At the other extreme is the fellow who stands on the soccer field. He's not very talented, but he dreams of making five goals this game. While he's dreaming about being the hero, he doesn't see the ball that another player passed to him and misses the goal he might have made!

The imagination is so fertile that it never seems to run out of nasty tricks. Another favorite ploy is offering us a stage where we can play out our anger or hostility or exploitation of another without having to take responsibility for the actual situation or the effects of our feelings. For example, someone makes a hurtful remark and I spend hours pounding the person in my imagination. I have no intention of carrying out my imaginative vendetta. I'd like to, but I fear the consequences. Neither do I want to deal creatively and positively with the problem, perhaps by talking to the person.

Similarly, after seeing a beautiful woman or a suggestive picture, I might imagine myself having sexual relations with her and even enjoy sexual arousal. I have no intention of acting out my desires, because it's impossible to do so, or because I fear the consequences, or because I'm afraid of what such an act might do to my reputation.

Even though this fantasy never becomes real, I create a certain reality in my imagination. And if I consciously choose to play out this sexual act in my imagination, I am abusing that person in my heart. Indeed, Jesus said that anyone who looks with lust at a woman has already committed adultery with her in his heart (Mt 5:28).

The imagination often plays on our fears. An oft-told childhood story tells of an acorn falling on Chicken Little's head. She panicked and ran around crying, "The sky is falling! The sky is falling!" A small thing can cause tremendous fear—if we allow the imagination to trick us by exaggerating the situation.

Parents naturally begin to worry when their children don't come home on time. An uncontrolled imagination can make the time of waiting unbearable. Often they can do nothing more at the time than surrender the child to God and to the care of Mother Mary.

Unfortunately, feuds and wars can begin or escalate because the collective imagination of one or both groups whips a single wrong into a cosmic cause. The imagination's tendency to exaggerate and create chaos led St. Teresa to call it "the crazy woman in the house."

We take a big step forward in becoming like Jesus and Mary

when we allow the Holy Spirit to take over our imagination and use it positively, letting his truth shine on its exaggerations and lies. Our Lord had a vivid imagination, as evidenced by the beautiful parables and stories he created. But Jesus also knew how to recognize the temptations of the father of lies. When Satan dramatized the attractive but deceptive roles of the false messiah—to turn stones into bread, to jump from the pinnacle of the temple, to obtain all the kingdoms of the world by worshiping Satan—Jesus rebuked his lies with the Scriptures.

Mary must have often found herself in situations where her imagination could have run riot. What did she think about when Jesus was lost for three days? What might she have thought about when he left home to begin his public ministry and wandered around "with no place to lay his head"? Or when she heard reports of the growing hostility of his enemies? We don't know the answers to those questions, but we can guess that, possessed by the Holy Spirit, she was able to surrender them to the Father as she learned to live with the unknown.

Exercises

- Consider the infinite imagination of God in creating the universe: the macrocosm of stars and planets, down to the microcosm of the tiniest bugs and atoms. Use Psalms 8 and 104.

- Consider how the devil tempted Jesus by playing on his imagination, showing him all the kingdoms of the earth and their glory, and how Jesus dispelled them by using the Word of God (Mt 4:8-10; Lk 4:5-8).

- Think of a time when you may have exaggerated an obstacle or a person's remark, and how you would now handle the same situation.

Steps on the Journey

1. How have you used your imagination creatively in the past? Does this indicate a gift you can use for the kingdom?

2. Think of a situation where your imagination ran wild, when perhaps you misread others' motives. How would you deal with a similar situation in the future?

3. How well do you live with the unknown? Can Mary be of help to you here? How?

Lord Jesus, I thank you for the gift of my imagination. I thank you that it reflects something of the Father's infinite creativity. Forgive me for not using it better. Forgive me for the times I have let it control me. Mary, teach me how to use my imagination for the glory of God and how to live with the unknown. Amen.

ELEVEN

Order in the Control Room: Transforming the Present

A FOCUSED MIND

WHILE RIDING HORSEBACK, St. Bernard and a friend were discussing prayer. St. Bernard admitted how easily his mind became distracted when he tried to pray. His friend, however, was not so humble. "I can pray for quite some time without being distracted," he boasted.

St. Bernard said in reply, "My friend, let us try saying one Hail Mary. If you can get through it without a distraction, I'll give you this horse."

"Agreed," said the friend, and he began to pray, "Hail Mary, full of grace... Bernard, does the saddle come with it?"

The faculty that holds our thoughts would be useless without the power of concentration by which we direct our minds to some worthwhile object and keep our attention focused there. Our objective is to put on the mind of Christ (Phil 2:5), to have the thoughts and attitudes of Jesus. This is not an easy task, but working at the healing of our memory and the disciplining of our imagination should eliminate some of the distractions from the past or the future.

If we love God with our whole heart, then we need to put our mind where our heart is. We may not always be thinking of God directly, but the activity of our mind should be at his service. That means our attention should be directed to whatever is good, lovely, beautiful, or useful for the kingdom: "Focus your minds on those things that are morally excellent and deserve praise: things that are true, honorable, right, pure, lovely to behold or to hear" (Phil 4:8).

What fills the mind is largely under our control. We can choose what books or magazines we read, what films we see, what music we hear. "I do not have time to read good books," a great man once said. "I have time to read only the best books." Many Christians don't guard their time so closely. They think they can read almost anything, see anything, listen to anything—and then find no difficulty in leading a good Christian life. If these people applied the same logic to their nutritional intake, they might say, "I can eat and drink anything without getting sick."

Those who are trying to follow and imitate Jesus need to ask, "What food for my mind will help me most to have the mind of Jesus?"

Intake of information is the first aspect of this "silence of the mind." The second is focus or concentration. To be able to "do what we are doing," to be fully present to the task of the moment, is already to be advanced in the spiritual life. People who are easily distracted at prayer usually have many distractions in everything they do. People who don't know how to focus their attention and energy on any one thing for very long are like butterflies flitting from one flower to another.

When Jesus visited Martha and Mary, Luke tells us that Martha was distracted with much serving. It wasn't that she was serving. But she was so anxious about what she was doing for her guest that she forgot the more important aspect of hospitality: listening to what her guest had to say. She was not focused the way Mary was. She could have prepared only "one dish" and spent the rest of the time listening to Jesus. We are often in the same situation: things that are really less important distract us from the central issue. At the wedding feast of Cana, on the other hand, the mother of Jesus was sufficiently focused to notice that the wine was running out. Her initiative saved the host from embarrassment and issued in "the first of Jesus' signs."

When I was young I used to daydream a lot. I spent an unbelievable number of hours living in the future or in the past or in some other place. Some of those fantasies were interesting and creative, but my daydreams rarely came to pass because I lived so little in the present. Learning about this virtue of focusing my mind was liberating. It was hard work at first, but I would consciously decide to *do what I'm doing*, giving my full attention to the work at hand. Concentrating on the task at hand did not exclude thinking about the past or the future. But when I did take a mental detour, I tried to do so consciously and not just float at sea without sail, paddle, or rudder.

As I worked at asserting control of my own thought life, I found strength in the truth that the only thing that is real is the *present*. The past is gone and the future is not here yet. The Lord is here—not somewhere else. Gradually I discovered more energy, joy, and enthusiasm for everything I did, for life itself. Negative thoughts, worries, and fears bothered me less and less. I became less distracted in prayer and more productive in general—all thanks to *silence of the mind*.

Meditations

Meditate on these Scriptures: Matthew 6:22; Philippians 2:5; 4:8; Ephesians 4:23; Colossians 3:16; Proverbs 14:30; 15:14.

THE HEART MOVES US TO ACTION

Jesus told his disciples, "Where your treasure is, there your heart will also be" (Mt 6:21). Our efforts to become aware of and assert control over our memory, imagination, and mind raise a nagging question: what role do our emotions play in memory, mind, and imagination?

St. Thomas called the passions, the emotions, the immediate source of our decisions and actions. The mind may show us what needs to be done, and the will may choose that course of action, but it is ordinarily the heart that moves us to action. Well-trained emotions respond more spontaneously to the good that is to be done; unruly passions prove more difficult to harness.

As with the previous area, the first stage in training our emotions is to become aware of them—not the feelings we *should* have but the ones we *do* have. Whether we are conscious of them or not, our feelings exert a profound influence upon our lives. The danger of remaining unaware of them is that we will be split between the self that is acting outwardly and the self that is feeling inwardly. I'm not suggesting that we must follow whatever emotion we have, but if the heart is not invested in our exterior actions, then we should try to change one or the other in order to become more authentic persons.

We sometimes ignore our real feelings, especially any "negative" ones, because we view them as bad or "unchristian." So we pretend we don't have them. But feelings serve an important function in our lives. They are like internal barometers telling us whether things are well or not in a certain part of our being.

Negative feelings, such as anger, act like a fuse in an electric line. When a short or overload hits the line, the fuse blows. We examine the line, repair the problem area, and then replace the fuse. If the fuse didn't warn us, the house might burn down. An emotional reaction in our relationship with someone warns us that something isn't working right. We had better pay attention to the problem before it explodes and ruins the relationship.

THE BIRTH OF FEELINGS

Before looking at the role emotions play in relationships, let's consider how they generally come about. There are usually three steps in the generation of feelings:

1. *An external event:* Something happens. I see an accident. I get sick. I fail an examination. Someone accuses me of something I didn't do.

2. *What I think about the event:* I view and interpret the event through a subjective lens. My thoughts—my self-talk concerning the event—stem from my system of values, my assumptions, convictions, and prejudices about life in general.

3. *The feeling itself:* My feelings are caused not so much by the event as by my way of interpreting or thinking about the event. Statements often make events responsible for feelings, for example, "Crowds make me nervous," or "He makes me angry." But that would assign events more control over my life than they actually have. I am responsible for my feelings and especially responsible for what I do with my feelings.

The event (step one) is like the tongue of a bell. The tone produced when it strikes the bell depends on the quality of the metal. The same tongue, transferred to a different bell, would produce a different sound. Thus two people may react to the same event differently, depending on their value system and inner emotional life. The news of Indira Gandhi's assassination was greeted with grief by the world and by most Indians, but some Sikh extremists rejoiced.

If our thoughts (step two) are reasonable and inspired by faith, they will be true, realistic, objective, and supported by evidence. Ideas of this kind will lead to healthy emotions. Self-talk can be implicit or hidden. I may ask myself questions: *Why me? How could this happen to me?* which really means, *This should never have happened!* Or, *What if they laugh at me?* means, *It would be terrible if they laughed at me!* Which means, *I wouldn't be able to bear it if they laughed at me.* Exclamations like "damn" or "hell" imply something like, *It's not fair,* or *This is terrible,* or *This should not have happened.*

Self-talk may be more explicit. If you consistently talk to yourself in terms of "should," "must," "have to," or "should not," instead of "want," "like," "desire," "prefer," then you may be trying to control something that is impossible to control. Also watch for words like "awful," "terrible," "unfair," "always," "never," "everyone," or blaming others with insulting words like "stupid," "idiot," "lamebrain," and so forth.

Our emotions (step three) stem primarily from our value system, that is, how we interpret the event (our self-talk) rather than the event itself. Thus we need to become aware of the self-talk we actually do and determine whether our thoughts are objectively true or distorted. A straight stick dipped in a pool of clear water will *look* broken. In the same way, an event interpreted by a mind given to distortion will be changed and the resulting emotions will be unhealthy.[1]

This complex intertwining of our thoughts and feelings shows how important the control of the mind, memory, and imagination is to achieving the silence of the heart. If our mind, memory, and imagination are filled with wholesome ideas, images, and memories, then our emotions become healthier. We could liken the heart to a plant. With proper sunlight, a plant can grow healthy and strong. Left in the dark, it will wither and die. So the heart needs to be exposed to the light of Christ, the light of faith and objective truth, if it is to grow. Left in the dark, it will wither and die.

FEELINGS AND RELATIONSHIPS

Now we turn to the chief area where feelings help us or get us into trouble: our relationships with others. Warm and positive feelings toward others strengthen relationships and help our love to be more complete and spontaneous. If our love for others is authentic, like God's, then it is impossible to love them too much. We may need to regulate our expressions of love according to what is appropriate, but if we really care for the other person, even restraint can be an act of love.

Our negative feelings toward others usually cause more problems. When something happens that makes us angry or frustrated with another person, we should take this feeling as a warning that something needs repair. Attending to relationship difficulties is especially important in family and community. Since a healthy and happy common life is built on strong, loving relationships, a breakdown in even one relationship can affect the whole community.

Let's consider our options when we feel angry or upset with someone.

We can try to handle our feelings in a number of *indirect* ways. If we don't want to involve the person at all, we can try to *release tension* by exercising, playing a game, taking a bath, going to a movie, plunging into work, going for a walk, taking an aspirin, taking a drink or drugs, or turning to sex. Obviously some of these are healthy ways to reduce tension, others are not. But none of them confronts the real problem head-on.

Another indirect way is to work out our anger through a *substitute outlet*. We might watch a violent movie or a boxing match and express our anger through these means. Or we could complain to others and seek sympathy.

A third indirect way is *displacement*. We slam the door or kick the dog instead of the person with whom we're angry. Or we explode at students or co-workers or family members. Another not uncommon way of displacement is to make ourselves the victim. We keep the anger inside and get more and more depressed. Internalized anger can even lead to suicide, which is a way of telling the offender, "Now look what you made me do."

Another indirect way of dealing with our feelings is by expressing anger *to the person*. Aggressive words, name calling, and snarls like "Shut up!" are likely to increase hostility in the other and in ourselves. We might pass judgment by saying things like, "You really wanted to hurt me, didn't you?" or "All you people are just alike." These are really statements about our own feelings, but we end up condemning others before they have a chance to explain themselves.

Another indirect but rather common reaction is *passive aggression*. Did you ever play on a sports team in your early years? Can you remember a time when you got angry at one or two other players and for the rest of the game you exerted minimum effort? You were in the game in body but everything else about you communicated that you weren't there. You didn't actually switch sides and play against your team as a member of the other team, but you played against your team as a member of *your* team.

This is called passive aggression. You were angry and acting out your aggression toward your own team, but you were doing it passively, by non-cooperation and minimum participation. It was your way of saying, "I'm very mad at you guys," but you didn't say so in words. You just acted like a sack of rice on the field. Family or community life or any common project can be seriously hampered if one or more members uses passive aggression. It is not a healthy way of handling our feelings.

The direct way of dialog. None of these indirect methods of working out relationships helps anyone deal with the real issue. Even more importantly, they usually increase hostility on both sides of the conflict. What is the best way? It is the *direct* way of *dialog*.

Direct dialog may not always be possible, but anyone living in a Christian family or community should be committed to this ideal. In doing so we take seriously what Jesus said: "If your brother does something to hurt you, go to him and show him his fault. But do it privately, just between your-selves" (Mt 18:15). Following is an outline of a procedure you could follow.

1. *Before the dialog, take some time for reflection.* In the presence of the Lord, ask yourself these questions:
    a. What am I feeling? Sad, angry, fearful, worried?
    b. Why? What causes me to feel this way?
    c. Shall I express the problem? How and when? (It is not always possible nor advisable to approach the person with whom you're having the problem. That person may be in a violent mood at the moment or may not be available. But ordinarily the sooner you can talk about a relationship problem the better. This keeps tensions from building up because of non-communication.)

2. *Pray for constructive attitudes:*
    a. I want to be reconciled for the other's sake, for my sake, for God's sake.
    b. I don't want to win an argument; I want to win a friend.
    c. I don't want to prove the other person wrong. I want to find out if I made a mistake and apologize. If I wasn't at fault, I want to give us both the opportunity to explain, forgive, and be reconciled.
    d. I don't want to demand that the other change, as if my happiness depended on the response. I simply

want to do what I need to do and leave the rest to God and to the other's free response.

3. *Helpful rules for the dialog itself.*

a. I should describe *my* feelings only. I shouldn't judge the other's motives. I shouldn't condemn or seek to take revenge or punish the other. I just *report* my feelings. For example, "Joe [or Mary], something happened at supper last night, which I would like to check out with you. When you (did or said)... I felt..." This statement gives the others the chance to explain and the freedom to admit their mistakes without having to defend themselves against attack.

b. Attack the problem, not the person. Assume that the other person will want to correct any problem in the relationship, and try to see the problem as one both of you could work on together.

c. Be specific: what word or behavior caused the problem? Not "You always seem to get upset when I bring up this topic...." But "Last night when I brought up this topic, you appeared to get upset, and I in turn got upset...."

d. One problem at a time: don't come with a litany of complaints about the other.

e. The change you desire in the other person should be reasonable and possible. You should also be willing to change if the dialog reveals your own behavior or reaction in a new light.

f. Good timing: usually the sooner the better, but not always.

g. The listener should repeat back to the other what he or she heard. Only when the other can say, "Yes, that's what I meant," can we be sure we understood the other.

h. Don't assume you know how the other person feels. Ask if necessary.

THE HEART OF JESUS AND MARY

Our work in these interior silences is all aimed at one goal: to have the heart of Jesus and Mary. We want to imitate Jesus not only outwardly, to do the works that he did, but we also want to experience his life inwardly, to have the emotions and the passions of Jesus himself. We want our outward actions—our work or study or play or service—to flow from a heart that has been transformed into Jesus' heart.

To reach this goal we need to learn and practice techniques of control—which means inner freedom not to be tossed about and governed by any passing thought or feeling. In addition we need to bathe our memory, our mind, our imagination, and our heart in the pure waters of the Holy Spirit, who is God's love.

Our Mother Mary is God's gift to help us gain the inner peace, serenity, and strength of her Son. Particularly is this true in dealing with our troublesome emotions. In October of 1984, I was attending a meeting in Rome, sitting in the back of a room listening to a talk on discernment based on St. Paul's Epistles. A Jesuit scholar was addressing about eighty persons who like myself were engaged in the formation of young religious. The lecture was flawless, without notes. The priest spent most of the time commenting on Philippians 1:9-11, a text that I had studied as part of my doctorate thesis many years earlier.

As I sat and listened to this impeccable presentation, I found myself mysteriously growing angrier and angrier. I was upset with myself for being angry, and this made me even more distressed. When later I was introduced to the speaker, I said a respectful "hello" and then left, still angry. I went to the chapel to pray and to take this overwhelming emotion to Mary. As I prayed she showed me why I was angry. The text he was expounding was one I knew by heart, and I could have done as good a job, I thought, as he—so why didn't they ask me to give the talk? More than that, two years earlier I had left a very successful life in the United States where I was a popular lecturer, as indeed the Jesuit was. Now I was a listener, a "nobody" lost in the crowd. I was also homesick for my former ministry back in the United States, even though I had chosen to leave for the mission in Nepal. The more I saw of this emotion, the more ashamed I was of it, but shame didn't get rid of the feeling. So I asked Mary what to do about it.

"All you need is a good cry," she said, almost audibly. And so it was. The anger and distress was simply the effect of unprocessed grief at what I had left behind. Two days later at communion time, we sang the Spanish hymn, *Pescador de Hombres* ("Fisher of men"), with the words, "There on the shore I have left my boat; with you, Lord, I will seek other seas." And the tears came and washed me clean. Mary is a good counselor when we are upset and don't know what to do.

Integrating our emotions is the work of a lifetime. I encourage you to return to these principles and exercises again and again in your spiritual journey.

Meditations

Undisciplined emotions or desires can be a source of great evil (Mt 15:19-20; Jas 4:1-2; Mt 5:28; Prv 11:23). We cannot be one with God unless we discipline our passions (Gal 5:24; 1 Jn 2:15-16). We must become passionate for God and for all that is good (Mt 5:8; 22:37-39; Prv 22:11).

Steps on the Journey

1. Reflect on one experience during the past week when you felt "out of control," when you had difficulty concentrating, when you felt you were ineffective. How would you respond if you encountered that situation again?

2. What kind of feelings or emotions most often disturb your inner peace? What events in your life have required near heroic efforts to remain peaceful? What daily aggravations have disturbed your inner silence?

3. Reflect on crisis situations in the life of Jesus and Mary: the flight to Egypt, the loss of Jesus in the temple, Jesus leaving home for his ministry, when Mary stood at the foot of the cross, when she accepted his broken body into her arms. Where did she find her strength? Ask her to show you.

"A clean heart create for me, O God..." (Ps 51:12) and give me the mind and heart of Jesus, filled with pure love of you and love of all. May you find in my heart an echo of the heart of Mary, who rejoiced at your wonders, whose every response was guided by your Holy Spirit. Amen.

TWELVE

The Inner Sanctuary

O UR EFFORTS TO TAKE HOLD of our outward communication and our inward faculties often reveal a significant degree of disorder. With awareness as the first fruit of our labors, our ultimate goal is to focus our energies and become truly present—to ourselves, to God, and to others. This is called *recollection*.

When people are genuinely present to us, they give us their undivided attention. They listen at a deeper level than just words or gestures; they pick up what lies hidden in our hearts. Sometimes they can identify our concerns better than we can. When they put into words what we've been thinking or feeling, we are amazed at their insight.

What enables a person to be present in this way? In a sense, the answer is very simple: focus. The person is able to screen out distractions, other emotions or concerns of the moment, and to concentrate all inner and outer energies on one point or individual.

We touched on this ability to focus our energies in discussing the "silence of the mind" in the previous chapter.

Now we look at the goal toward which all the silences converge—presence or recollection. The purpose of all the silences is to enable us to be recollected, that is, focused so as to be totally available to the person or the task at hand.

THE POINT OF RECOLLECTION

Many people enter adulthood retaining the brief attention span of children. As students they have trouble concentrating either on an assignment or a classroom lecture. At work they frequently make mistakes because their thoughts wander. When conversing with someone, they're often thinking about something or someone else "more important" than the person with whom they're speaking.

These distractible types belong neither to themselves nor to anyone or anything else. They are captives of the first attraction that crosses their senses or the loudest emotion that clamors to be heard. Naturally these individuals will bring to prayer the same tendencies. If those who are disciplined struggle to remain focused in prayer, imagine how impossible it is for those who are habitually distracted.

We are often tempted to consider the present person or task or object to be less important than other options. We want to get done with *this* in order to get on with *that*. This approach inevitably creates inner tension. We may find it particularly difficult to give our full attention to someone who interrupts us—whether in person or by phone.

If we cannot be present in this way, we need to decide whether we can reschedule a time to adequately address the individual's need, or whether we can take the interruption as a reordering of our schedule and deal with the person then and there. In the latter case, we need to let go of any impatience we might feel at being interrupted and try to focus totally on the person at hand.

On his way to Jairus' house, Jesus was interrupted by a woman who had suffered a flow of blood for twelve years. By graciously accepting the interruption and healing the woman, Jesus showed us that interruptions can be God's way of revealing his agenda when we're preoccupied with our own.

Besides interruptions, we can also be thrown off track by

distractions of the mind, painful memories, fantasies about what might happen in the future, or emotional reactions to recent events. We know we need to move ahead with the task at hand, or with our prayer time, but a disturbance in one of our faculties blocks us from doing so.

Recollection teaches us to use the faculties over which we have some control to subdue the ones which are disturbed. For example, if we're very upset, taking a walk (using our body) may help us to calm down. If someone has hurt us, we may know that confronting the feeling and making a decision in the heat of the moment isn't the best option. So we plunge into some other activity as a way to temporarily distance ourselves from the initial impact. Later, when our emotions aren't so overwhelming, we can reflect and pray about the matter. Illicit sexual fantasies that bombard the imagination can often be diverted by occupying ourselves with some creative activity of the mind.

When we can "do what we're doing" and live fully in the present moment, we will be able to know the presence of God and the presence of others—because we are first present to ourselves! When we reach this point of recollection, our inner being becomes more than a *control room;* it becomes an *inner sanctuary.* For God is not found in distractions. Nor is he found through escape from the task at hand or the person at hand. Rather it is *in* and *through* the present task or object or person that God reveals himself.

A saint was once asked, "What is the most important moment in life?" The saint wisely answered: "The present moment." The past is no longer real, except in memory. The future is not yet here. We have only the present moment. That is where we find life. And that is where we find God.

In attaining recollection Mary can be a great help. The mere serenity of her face, portrayed in so many paintings, can give us some idea of the peace and presence the Holy Spirit would work in us if we drew near to her. Hers is not stoic impassiveness. It is rather the inner strength that comes from having her whole being centered on God in the present moment. In her home at Nazareth, that might have meant total availability to the person or need she was confronted with at the moment. During the time of her pregnancy Mary was always aware of the divine child in her womb: "Can a mother forget her baby, or a woman the child within her womb?" (Is 49:15). Yet she was able to be totally present to her cousin Elizabeth because that was where God in the present moment was to be found. When we are inwardly disturbed, a glance at our mother can calm the storm or at least suggest the first steps toward dealing with it.

Meditations

"Be still and know that I am God" (Ps 46:11). "God is in its midst; it shall not be disturbed" (Ps 46:6; see also Is 30:15). We must love God with all our faculties (Dt 6:5). God speaks to the heart in solitude (Hos 2:16; Lk 3:2, 4:1). The peace of God is beyond understanding (Phil 4:7). We are to live in the presence of God (Gn 17:1).

Steps on the Journey

1. Have you ever tried using one faculty to gain better control of another? Was it effective? How could it be more so?

2. What does the word "presence" mean to you? How are you "present" to others in a way that makes Jesus' love and mercy present to them?

3. Reflect on some specific things you can do to bring the presence of Jesus to others when they're in turmoil. Do you bring a sense of calm when others are frenzied? Do you bring a sense of caring when others feel no one cares about them? A sense of hope when others are depressed?

4. Have you tried looking at Mary when you need to "pull yourself together" or deal with some inner disturbance?

Father, make my heart a sanctuary where your Spirit dwells. I wish to be one with Jesus, whose heart and will are always one with yours. Mother Mary, teach me your serenity. In those moments of inner storm give me wisdom and discernment so that I may use the challenge of the moment to find peace and find God. Amen.

THIRTEEN

Mastering the Circumstances

YOU WAKE UP ONE MORNING to find you've overslept. No time for breakfast brings on a throbbing headache. You rush to your car to no avail: the battery is dead. A neighbor offers to jump start your car but spends ten minutes looking for his battery cables. Much to your chagrin, you arrive at work late, hoping to forget the day's rough start.

You soon discover that the job someone else was supposed to have done yesterday didn't get done, a goof for which the boss blames you. At lunch time someone spills coffee on your new suit. The drive home from work doesn't go much better: traffic has been slowed to a snail's pace by an accident. As your car inches forward on the expressway, you remember a poster you once saw, "The hurrieder I go, the behinder I get."

Would this string of troubles ruin your day? For many people it would. By the end of the day they would be in a terrible mood. If you asked them for a simple favor, they might bark at you like a dog. Yet some people would manage to keep fairly calm in the midst of these problems. Some might even begin to laugh at the ridiculous pile of frustrations. They might identify with Charlie Brown and see the humorous side of this "child's garden of reverses."

THE COMPANION OF OUR MISERIES

Who or what is responsible for our happiness, our peace, our joy? If we depend on external events or circumstances to make us happy, we're going to be frustrated daily because we have little or no control over external events. But we do have some control, and therefore some responsibility, over how we respond to events and circumstances—certainly our behavioral response and, to some extent, our emotional response.

We discussed at some length in chapter eleven how our feelings sometimes get the better of us and how we can handle them more effectively. How we respond to an event depends on how we interpret that event (our self-talk, the way we think about it), and this interpretation also affects our feelings. Before leaving the taking-hold virtues, we need to consider two external challenges that may attack our inner control. The first concerns annoying or painful circumstances, the topic of this chapter. The second is the challenge of obedience, which we will discuss in the next chapter.

Allowing ourselves to be controlled by events and circumstances can be a major obstacle to our spiritual freedom and growth. And it certainly can paralyze a community in its mission or rob a family of its peace. I'm not referring to heavy duty trials such as persecution for the faith, or being whipped or starved or exiled from our people like many Christians in other countries. I mean the simpler, more immediate daily crosses which everyone experiences. Those who are soft will crumble under these difficulties, small though they be.

The books of Exodus and Numbers describe how the people of Israel were freed from slavery to the Egyptians by a mighty, saving act of God. After their dramatic escape, the Israelites found themselves in the desert and soon discovered that they missed the rich food and comforts they had enjoyed in Egypt. Some would have preferred to return to slavery in order to enjoy those comforts. Many of the Hebrews complained at the food the Lord gave them in the desert.

Have you ever tried to lead a group of children on an out-ing? If so, you know how quickly they grow tired or bored, how quickly they begin to complain about anything uncom-fortable—the weather is too hot or too cold; they can't wait to reach a source of water. Their patience, like their attention span, is very limited. Children want immediate satisfaction of their needs. As they become adults many of them learn how to wait to have their needs gratified. But when adults try to form community for a mission, the task often triggers the same weaknesses, which the Bible simply calls "complaining."

Life is full of ups and downs, hills and valleys, high points and low points. At certain times we may experience a high that is very high, or a low that is very low. But usually every day brings a moderate share of ups and downs. When the Buddha looked at human life and saw the large amount of suf-fering, he searched for a way out of it. He concluded that human desires were the cause of suffering, and that the way to peace of mind was to get rid of all desires.

We do not see the same philosophy in Jesus, either in his own life or in his teaching. He does tell us not to worry about tomorrow (Mt 6:34) and he does surrender to the Father's will (Mk 14:36), but only after a struggle in prayer. Jesus is a deeply passionate man. He manifests zeal for his Father's house and expresses anger at oppression of the poor and out-cast. He weeps at the tomb of Lazarus. And his call to his dis-ciples is "Come, follow me." We discover untold joys and excitement in that following, but we also find the cross.

Jesus was a Jew, and Jews were passionate people. Their prayers, as we see so clearly in the Psalms, were full of desires, hopes, fears, frustrations, which they used as fuel for their peti-tions. From the time of Abraham, they believed in a God who cares, who addresses them with his word, his call, and his demands. He is a God who gets involved with them by making a covenant and calling them his people. He sees their miseries in Egypt and intervenes to save them. And he is the compan-ion of their later history in the desert, in the promised land,

and even in the exile. When they long for a Messiah, he is described as Emmanuel, God with us. That is who Jesus is: the *companion* of our miseries, God who saves us by totally sharing our human sufferings.

Mary is often portrayed as so serene that we wonder if anything ever bothered her. But this is a projection of a stoic image onto a woman who was a strong and passionate Jewish mother. The mysteries of her life, which we ponder in the rosary, are titled precisely, "the joyful, the sorrowful, the glorious." She walked "by faith and not by sight" (2 Cor 5:7). In her faith journey, the circumstances of her life at times might well have been overwhelming: birthing her Son in a stable; fleeing Herod who wanted to kill her child; losing Jesus in the temple; fearing that the people of Nazareth would throw him over the cliff when he returned home during his ministry; standing at the foot of the cross and watching her only Son die. But if she was the typical Jewess, she knew how to process her feelings through the psalms. She knew how to conquer the circumstances by clinging to the God of victory. She was not a reed easily blown over by the slightest breeze. Like the ideal woman of Proverbs, she was "clothed with strength and dignity" and because of her faith she could laugh at the obstacles life threw her way (Prv 31:25).

DEALING WITH ANNOYANCES

Can we realistically expect to find some formula, some secret by which we can make the valleys of our lives disappear? No. We would become inhuman, and certainly not like Jesus or Mary. But as we grow more like them, the sinful sources of our sufferings will diminish. Our suffering will be caused less by the simple annoyances and discomforts and more by the injustices done to others, the sufferings of the poor, the violence in the world.

At whatever stage of growth we find ourselves, the key for the Christian response to sufferings, great or small, is this: we never need experience them alone. We have a companion for the journey: it is Jesus. If we are high, let us rejoice with Jesus; if we are low, let it be with Jesus, who knows how we feel and will help us carry the cross if we let him. This, after all, was Mary's joy—to be with Jesus in everything. And Mary accompanies us along the way. The thought of her presence can intensify our joys and lighten our sorrows.

When I was a barefoot child I remember stepping on a nail. I ran to my mother who treated it but more importantly reassured me that this was not the end of the world, that I would survive, that I could let go of the fear that traumatized me. As adults we don't run to our natural mothers that way any more, but we do remain children of the kingdom, and we have a mother who can reassure us that with God all will turn to good and we can be more than conquerors because of him who loved us (Rom 8:28-37).

What stabilizes life for the Christian is not the suppression of feelings or desires but companionship with Jesus and Mary. That is why Jesus tells his disciples to rejoice always, especially when they are persecuted for his sake. That is why Peter and John could go forth from the Sanhedrin rejoicing that they had been counted worthy to suffer for the name of Jesus. That is why many of the martyrs sang as they were being led to execution. It is why St. Thomas More, on the way to being beheaded, could joke with his executioner, "When you swing the sword, please don't cut my beard. It has not committed treason!"

The secret of this amazing joy was knowing that they were with Jesus and he with them, the same Jesus who said, "My joy no one can take from you." Read Romans 8 in this light, especially the last half of the chapter. If we can endure serious suffering as Jesus' disciples, surely he will give us strength to handle our little annoyances.

Meditations

Consider the example of Jesus (1 Pt 2:20-25; Heb 12:2; Is 53:7). Consider the example of the apostles as well (Acts

5:41). Also see the following Scriptures (Prv 16:32; Ps 119:71; Mt 5:39; 1 Cor 13:4, 7).

Exercise

• Take some quiet time of reflection and make a list of things that normally upset you. Why does each one upset you? How does it affect your behavior? Now take each of those events or things or situations to prayer and ask how you would like to handle them in the future. How would you do it if you were really convinced that Jesus and Mary were with you? Conclude with reading Romans 8:18-39.

Steps on the Journey

1. You may wish to share reflections on your experience of the exercise given above.

2. What does "mastering the circumstances" mean to you? Mastering can mean: controlling, rising above, coping, overcoming. How would you describe Jesus' attitude toward this virtue? How do you think he was able to master the circumstances of his public life and ministry?

3. How do you handle interruptions? How would Mary handle them?

"In all these things we are more than conquerors because of him who loved us." Jesus, convict me more and more of the truth of that word. Show me how to stand above the circumstances. Teach me to praise you in all things and at all times (Ps 34:2), especially when things go wrong. Mary, remind me that Jesus has won the victory and help me to claim it. Amen.

FOURTEEN

Interdependent Cooperators

S OME YEARS AGO Ford Motor Company used advertisements showing a light bulb being switched on, accompanied by the words, "Ford has a better idea." God has a better idea for our lives than we have. If we follow God's way as illuminated by the light of Christ, we will find greater joy and happiness than we could ever find on our own.

Unfortunately, something within us resists this notion of accepting someone else's plan for our lives. We want to do it our way. We want to run our own show. We admire the rugged individualist, the Lone Ranger who saves the town single-handedly. Cooperating with someone who has different ideas looks like giving in, and giving in looks like weakness.

The kingdom of God is not built by lone rangers. It is not built by *independent operators* but by *interdependent coopera-tors:* people cooperating with others and cooperating with God. "Thy will be done" immediately follows "Thy kingdom come" in the Lord's prayer. God's will is his kingdom. If we want to build his kingdom, we must do his will.

Surely Mary models obedience in accepting her vocation and all its consequences in her life—at the annunciation, in the journey to Bethlehem, in fulfilling the laws of pilgrimage with Joseph, in companioning her Son to the cross. Yet, even more importantly, she directs those who would be the Lord's servants to "do whatever he tells you" (Jn 2:5). In this she fulfills the role of Lady Wisdom who repeatedly counsels obedience to the Lord (Prv 8:20; Sir 24:22). If we have chosen to put ourselves under Mary's guidance, then we will hear her saying to us, on the eve of every important decision in our lives, "Do whatever he tells you."

Modern abuses of authority have rendered the virtue of obedience suspect. Consider the "blind obedience" of the Nazi underlings to their leaders which resulted in so much suffering and death. What can we understand about obedience to God's will as it is revealed to us through the events of our lives, through other persons, and through the inspirations of the Holy Spirit?

MEDIATED THROUGH COVENANT

In the New Testament, Mary was the first to say yes to the Lord. But, as we have seen, her fiat involved many other assents to events and to people: to Joseph, to the authorities, to the prompting of the Holy Spirit to visit Elizabeth, and to the temple rituals. Likewise Jesus was obedient, first to his parents (Lk 2:51) and then to the Father's plan for his ministry, which ended in his suffering and death on the cross. His disciples did the Father's will by following Jesus during his public ministry. After Christ's resurrection and the sending of the Holy Spirit, God's will was revealed through the community and "the teaching of the apostles" (Acts 2:42).

We can see in these examples that God's will is ordinarily mediated to us through other people. This mediation is based on a covenant, primarily God's covenant with us in Jesus. God has permanently committed himself to us in Jesus, and we by our "obedience of faith" (Rom 1:5) and baptism have committed ourselves to him irrevocably. This implies an obedience to the Word of Jesus, to his commandments (Jn 14:15).

Within that universal covenant, however, God has ordained other covenants. For many, this is marriage. Marriage in Christ means a mutual submission of one to the other (Eph 5:21).[1] It means a willingness to give up personal preferences for the good of the other and the family. Spouses find their personal fulfillment in the gift of self to the other. Marriage is not a fifty-fifty agreement but a 100 percent gift on the part of both husband and wife.

As a consequence of this sacramental covenant, each spouse agrees that no important decision will be made without input from the other. Thus the obedience of faith finds a concrete expression in the mutual obedience of one marriage partner to the other. In practice, this often means holy compromise, preferring to do something the other person's way for the sake of unity.

Christian communities are also based to some degree on covenant. This commitment is clearest in religious communities, where the individual by vow commits himself or herself to seek God's will in and through the community. And each community has certain structures (general or provincial chapters, councils, superiors) through which the will of God is sought and agreed upon.

One example of how this works comes from my own life. After ten years of successful teaching at St. Mary's University, I got a call from my Provincial (on Good Friday!), asking me if I would be willing to move to St. Louis to take the job of rector of the Marianist seminary there. He was kind and wise enough to give me time to think and pray about it. My vow of obedience meant that I would accept any assignment given to me. That's what the "community covenant" of religious vows means. But it doesn't mean that obeying is always easy. It took some prayer and reflection to bring myself to an inner acceptance of the external call, for I was very comfortable where I was and my Provincial was asking me to risk going into the unknown. I didn't want to say "yes" grudgingly or do the job halfheartedly. That's where I had to pray, asking Jesus and Mary to give me the ability to say "yes" in my heart as well as on my lips. I did. And so began a new chapter of grace in my life.

Besides religious communities such as mine, we have also seen the establishment of another kind of Christian community, sometimes called "intentional communities," where basic agreements or "covenants" form the foundation for a shared life. These structures are used to agree on major directions and decisions. In daily community living, however, everyone must practice a lot of "give and take," show a genuine concern for the common good, and know the value of holy compromise.

SECULAR COVENANTS

Even civic society presumes a covenantal relationship of sorts. We agree to abide by the legitimate laws of the land, and the civil government in turn is bound to protect our safety. Though he could have exempted himself as above human authority, Jesus submitted to the laws of the land (Mt 17:24-27). And the first letter of Peter urges us to civil obedience as a way of witnessing to the gospel (1 Pt 2:13-17). Joseph and Mary obeyed the census decree and went to Bethlehem, perhaps unaware at the time that they would thus fulfill God's plan for the birth of the Messiah as foretold by Micah 5:1.

There are exceptions to this, of course, as in the case of unjust laws. Jesus himself at times broke the rules that he considered humanly oppressive. Many early Christians were martyred because they refused to submit to the decrees that commanded worship of the Emperor and the Roman gods. Today many Christians feel they must risk arrest to protect the lives of the unborn, just as Martin Luther King did to gain civil rights for the oppressed. But in our ordinary daily lives, obedience to established authority is a way of obeying God himself.

That doesn't mean that we never question a superior's decision or instruction. In fact, one element of covenant loyalty requires that we bring to the attention of those in authority facts they may not know or perhaps haven't weighed sufficiently, so their decision can be better informed. Nor does obedience mean that we must consider what we've been told to do as the best decision in every circumstance. What it does mean is that, once we have respectfully intervened and discerned that the command is not against the law of God, for the sake of order we carry out the directive, trusting that God will use it ultimately for good.

In our places of work, our willingness to cooperate with others creates an atmosphere of mutual support and creativity. This ordinarily produces better work results, but more importantly our cooperation bears witness that the gospel of love holds the answer to even the deepest needs of the earthly city. If obedience of this kind feels like bondage to us, perhaps we need to ask ourselves whether we are not victims of a greater bondage such as pride, self-will, or arrogance. The Word of God tells us that true freedom is to be found in becoming slaves of God (1 Pt 2:16) and in putting ourselves at the service of others (Gal 5:13).

Meditations

Consider the obedience of Jesus (Lk 2:51; Jn 4:34; 12:49; 14:30-31; 19:11). Meditate on the obedience of Mary (Lk 1:38). Ponder the obedience of faith to which we are all called (Rom 1:5; Jn 14:15). Reflect on obedience to those in authority or those with whom we have a special relationship that sometimes calls for obedience: the authority of the apostles, the church (Acts 2:42; Lk 10:16; Heb 13:17); in marriage (Eph 5:21); at work (Col 3:23-24).

Exercise

• Set aside one day at work or at home to resolutely practice cooperation in thought and action, no matter what comes up. What differences do you see in yourself or in others?

Steps on the Journey

1. Do you find it hard to cooperate with others? Do you always insist that your way of doing things is better? Are you willing to compromise for the sake of the common good?

2. Do you have a problem with authority figures? If so, where does this come from? Is it due to anger with your parents or older siblings at home? What would Jesus or Mary do in a situation like this?

3. How can you unselfishly cooperate with others: in your relationships, at home, at work, school, community, group?

4. Jesus' disciples often got in the way of his purposes because they wanted to be first. Do you remember moments from your life when you did the same? (It's easier to talk about our selfish moments in childhood, and harder to admit what we have done as adults.)

Teach me, O Lord, to do your will. Show me those roadblocks I erect against your plan for my life. Let me see those you have placed in my life not as competitors but as team members, persons with whom I need to cooperate and support in order that the kingdom may come more fully. Don't allow me to be so attached to my ideas and my ways of doing things that I cannot yield to others.

Mary, you found God in simple obedience to his call in your life. You also sought to make a family of your Son's disciples in the upper room, as you had helped to form the Holy Family at Nazareth. May I seek to do the same with the companions the Father has given me on my journey. When I am tempted to follow my own lights instead of God's, may I hear your voice, "Do whatever he tells you." Amen.

Part Three

Letting Go

Letting Go

Bringing our communication and our inner life under the control of the Holy Spirit looks like a life-time project. And so it is. Our first attempts at least make us more aware of our inner tendencies and our need for deeper conversion.

Our turbulent struggle to gain better control of ourselves reveals the presence of deeper attachments which cause the surface disturbance. Hurricanes are not born out of nothing. When the ocean water reaches a certain degree of warmth, it spawns tropical storms. God wants to sanctify us to our very depths: "May the Lord sanctify you through and through, and may your whole being, spirit, soul, and body, be preserved blameless for the coming of our Lord Jesus with all his holy ones" (1 Thes 5:23).

Being sanctified in our deepest parts, however, goes beyond "taking hold." We don't know our inner depths very well, and certainly we exert only minimal control over what psychologists call our unconscious. Here we need more than ever the action of the Holy Spirit, for this work of purification is ultimately something only he can do. We have the assurance, of course, that he wants to do this and will do it if we give him permission.

This part involves not so much "taking hold" as "letting go." As the Holy Spirit reveals to us the things to which we cling, he offers us the grace to loosen our grasp. Letting go tends to be more frightening than grasping for control—more like trusting a swimming instructor who tells us to relax and to let the water hold us up.

While scary, the Lord's invitation to trust marks our progress. It signals that our relationship with him is becoming the most significant dynamic in our lives. And this is all according to God's plan. For we discover that our perfection is less important to him than is our trust. In fact, it is our trust that enables God to take over more of the work of perfecting us.

The Bible is filled with examples of this invitation to trust God's leading and his action. Jesus invites Peter to walk on the water, trusting his Lord (Mt 14:22-33); one day he will be led where he would rather not go (Jn 21:18). Abraham was led out, not knowing where the Lord was taking him (Heb 11:8). The Good Shepherd leads us even in the dark valley (Ps 23:4). The good branches on the Vine will be pruned (Jn 15:2).

Mary was given God's own Son to hold in her womb, in her arms, in her home. But she also knew painful moments of letting him go—all the more painful because of the deep love with which she had cherished him. Her ultimate letting go was at the cross when she let go of Jesus for the last time. That is why she is a good counselor when we discover some attachment that, unlike her loving attachment to Jesus, is rooted in our unredeemed ego.

A personal example of letting go comes to mind. "[B]uy from me gold refined by fire" (Rv 3:18). These words of Jesus in the Book of Revelation jumped out at me one morning during prayer. In the context of speaking to the church of Laodicea, the Lord was presenting this as a remedy for lukewarmness in his service. *What is that pure gold?* I asked. Then I realized it is Jesus' own love that has been made pure through the fire of his passion, his total gift of self. And he was offering it to me.

But Jesus also said, "Buy it." My next questions were, *How do I buy it? What price do I have to pay?* And I realized I had to let go of something and turn it over to the Lord.

At the time, I was harried by all the demands made on me and my time. I was feeling angry and resentful in the face of too many requests. I wrote in my journal, "But it is not the fault of others for begging of my time and ministry. The fault is mine for being so attached to my image that I feel I must say yes to every request. And I get angry with people for asking because it puts me in the dilemma of saying no and disappointing them (looking somewhat less in their eyes) or saying yes and taking on the job as another burden." Jesus was asking me to let go of my image as a people-pleaser.

A young woman student of mine was a great runner. She had won all kinds of medals and was aiming for the Olympics. Then she had an accident which permanently injured her back. This talented young woman shared with me her struggle to let go of her "Plan A" and to find God and a new life in "Plan B."

A more common example concerns parents who eventually must let go of the children they have reared. For each of us, the ultimate letting go is death, so that the Lord can bring us into the glory he has promised. And we are prepared for that final release by thousands of little moments of letting go as we journey.

In the next six chapters, we will look at various obstacles to our personal and corporate growth in Christ: three *interior* challenges, then three obstacles of an *external* nature—all of which provide opportunities to find our strength in God and to trust his purifying action in our lives.

FIFTEEN

Strength in Weakness

IF WE EVER ENTERTAIN THE IDEA that we're omnipotent, the illusion doesn't last long. We soon come face to face with our limitations as finite creatures. We can't do everything.

We are also wounded creatures, which limits us even more. Some face more obvious limitations: the deaf, the blind, the crippled, the retarded, the autistic. But those who enjoy wellness and success in life—even the weight-lifter, the beauty queen, the marathon winner, the CEO—have their limitations as well, in some ways all the more confining because not so obvious and therefore more easily covered over. The weight-lifter may fear to speak in public; the beauty queen may hold a deep grudge; the CEO may have a drinking problem. We usually avoid certain situations which would reveal our weakness. For instance, a person who is shy will do anything to escape getting up in front of a group. Someone who is clumsy at dancing will try to relate in other ways. Someone who fears rejection will avoid confronting certain people.

When we compare ourselves with those who seem more gifted, we can become overwhelmed with our limitations and begin to devalue our self-worth. One way to overcome this tendency is to affirm our own gifts. A better way is to realize that God has made each of us as unique beings precisely because he loves us. He calls each of us to a unique mission in this world and a unique glory in his kingdom. God doesn't make junk and he doesn't make clones. When he made you, like everyone else, he threw away the mold!

In the early years of my life, I grew in self-worth by developing gifts I knew I had. I was the youngest of four boys. My eldest brother was a gifted "fiddler" and became a pilot instructor; my next older brother was an excellent calf-roper and hunter; brother number three used to perform as a trick-roper and later became a Marine pilot. They were five to eight years older than I. I just couldn't compete with them, and besides my interests lay elsewhere. So I developed my writing skills and at age eleven began my own newspaper. I pushed the intellectual and spiritual development of my talents all the way through my religious life, ordination to the priesthood, professorship, and even the writing of books. All of this gave me a sense of worth.

But it wasn't enough. In fact, the incessant push to achieve ultimately led to a crash—burnout and emotional exhaustion. And it was when I hit bottom that I found the Lord in a new way. It was as if he had to break me before I could see that my worth had to come from a deeper source than my achievements. That period of weakness turned out to be one of the greatest blessings of my life. I discovered, however imperfectly, what Paul meant when he said, "Strength is made perfect in weakness." I began to trust the Lord more than I had before, and that became a source of new strength.

I still sometimes get anxious before a big challenge, especially when I am going to have to deal with an individual or group where I anticipate conflict. Little by little I'm learning to leave this anxiety in the hands of Mary, accepting ahead of time even the possibility of failure, and often she works miracles!

YOUR FAVORITE FEARS

Most of us don't need to be convinced of our weaknesses. We know them all too well. But if we don't know what they are, or if we want to know them better, we can ask ourselves: "What am I afraid of?" Fear is often a response to feelings of inadequacy or weakness. What situations paralyze you, block you from being yourself and doing all the good you could do for God?

Usually each of us struggles with one fear more than others. It could be something like fear of crowds, fear of angry people, fear of heights, fear of rejection, or fear of loneliness. In a retreat some years ago I asked the participants to list their favorite fears. We wrote them on the chalkboard and ended up with over a hundred.

What if we didn't have these fears and weaknesses? We could do so much more for God and for others. But even when we try, we find we cannot overcome them by our own power. Like Paul's thorn in the flesh, certain weaknesses may be with us until we die. But also like Paul, we too can hear the Lord say, "My grace is sufficient for you, for power is made perfect in weakness" (2 Cor 12:9). In other words, God can use our weaknesses to demonstrate his power.

How do we get this to happen? By trust. Instead of dwelling on what we can't do because of our weakness, we look at what God can do through us if we lean on him. Instead of looking at the wind and the waves, we keep our eyes fixed on Jesus. And he empowers us to walk on the waters.

When I was in Nepal I met a young Irishman with black hair and a beard. His face was somewhat distorted, and one ear was completely missing. "I was born a thalidomide baby," he explained. "But God has so blessed me that in return I decided to sell my car and use the money to pay my way to India to work with Mother Teresa and the dying people in Calcutta."

This young man could have used his disability as a permanent crutch through life. Instead, by letting go and dwelling on God's blessing, he was able to do much more than his natural condition would lead us to expect.

Dealing with our weaknesses is a form of risk, and risk is a form of letting go. Jesus risked everything, including his life, to achieve the mission the Father gave him. The Gospels suggest that Mary's life was full of risks. Saying "yes" to the angel meant risking that Joseph would divorce her, or that her people would reject her for apparent adultery. She risked rejection at Cana when she intervened to ask Jesus to change his timetable for beginning his public ministry. What enabled her to take one risk after another? Clearly an incredible trust in God.

Meditations

In the Lord I can do all things (Phil 4:13). God chooses the weak to shame the strong (1 Cor 1:27). "When I am weak, then I am strong" (2 Cor 12:9-10). God uses weakness in our ministry (2 Cor 13:4-5). See also these Scriptures: Psalm 40:4; 125:1; Jeremiah 17:5.

Exercises

- In prayer, ask yourself what situation makes you freeze up or withdraw. Bring this to the Lord, ask his help. Then, with his grace, see yourself acting differently. Refashion your inner image of yourself as you think God would like you to be (and as you would like yourself to be). When you find yourself in that same situation again, recall your new image and act accordingly.

- In a group that you trust, suggest that each person share a dominant fear. Then ask the group to pray with you for deliverance from that fear and an empowering of God's grace to be strong in that area.

- Reflect on Mary's response to situations in her life when she had to face some fearsome circumstances: for example, when she and Joseph looked for a room in the inn right before Jesus' birth and when they had to flee in the middle of the night to Egypt. How do you think her confidence in

God sustained Mary in her weakest moments? How does confidence in God's plan for your life sustain you during times when you are fearful?

Steps on the Journey

1. What instances in the life of Jesus show his trust in the Father in moments of difficulty or weakness?

2. What instances in the life of Mary show her trust in God and willingness to risk?

3. What have you found most helpful when you are confronted with a task that seems beyond you? Think of instances.

4. Have you seen miracles in your life at moments when you put your trust in Jesus and called on Mary's help?

> Lord Jesus, teach me that my weaknesses need not be my enemies if I will only turn them over to you. For you love to choose the weak to confound the strong. You have chosen me, and so I rejoice even now that my weakness can reveal your glory. Mary, it is a mother's role to give most attention to her weakest children. Help me to find God's strength in my very weakness. Amen.

SIXTEEN

Weakness in Strength

D URING THE HUNGARIAN REBELLION of 1956, the International Red Cross pleaded for blood in massive amounts to help the victims of the war. I was studying at our international Marianist Seminary in Fribourg, Switzerland, at the time. A large number of the seminarians went down to the university gym, where some fifty beds had been installed for the blood drive.

Among our group was Francisco, a lean Spaniard who was small of stature. At his side loomed Juan, a muscular giant. The contrast couldn't have been greater, even in the gait with which they approached the gymnasium. Francisco trod with uncertainty, scarcely disguising his dread of blood and needles. Juan sauntered along, casually telling jokes to his fellow seminarians.

After each of us had donated his pint of blood, we were all given a cup of hot chocolate. Noticing that Francisco looked "green around the gills," Juan began to tease and ridicule the "softy." But in the very midst of his finger-pointing and teasing, Juan paled, his eyes closed, and he fainted into the arms of Francisco. His momentary collapse brought laughter from everyone—including Juan himself after he revived.

WHAT STRENGTHS DO WE BRING TO THE JOURNEY?

I have often thought of Juan's blustering behavior as an illustration of another tendency to which human nature is prone: presumptuous overconfidence in self. It is weakness concealed as strength.

Recent personality studies suggest that each individual possesses an area of strength, which in itself is a gift, but one that can easily lead a person to excess and ultimately to self-destruction. For example, perfectionists are never satisfied with themselves or others. This drive for perfection can lead them to sanctity, but it can also drive them and the people who have to live with them crazy! Those who excel in caring for others can expend themselves to the point of burn-out. Goal-oriented executives can accomplish great things—and die young of a heart attack. People who like to work can become workaholics.

One of my strengths is a passion for using time well. I am project-oriented, and I like to get things done even before a deadline. This strength has enabled me to accomplish a lot. But I've also become aware that the project at hand can become more important than people—those involved in the project or those who interrupt. Those involved can get the impression that I'm interested in them only insofar as they can help with the project. Those who interrupt can sense by my tone of voice or body language that I'm annoyed at the interruption, or that I want to hurry along and send them on their way.

These strength-tendencies are all the more seductive because we ordinarily repress danger signals. Our strength and our momentum push us on to seemingly greater heights. Then we exceed our limits and end up hurting ourselves and others.

Two weeks after getting her driver's license, a high school student I know took a sharp turn on a country road and skidded on loose gravel. The accident totaled the new pickup and nearly killed her and her passenger.

"But I was only going thirty miles an hour," the girl explained to her father.

"But what did the sign say?" he asked.

"Fifteen," she admitted.

This novice driver had ignored the danger signal. We tend to do the same with our strengths, especially those which appear to be very virtuous.

Peter provides an outstanding example of someone who relied on his own strength and repeatedly fell on his face. He boasted that even if all the other disciples abandoned Jesus, he would never deny him. Yet deny Christ he did, three times.

Shakespearean protagonists such as Hamlet and Macbeth always possessed some tragic flaw in an otherwise powerful personality—flaws that ultimately led to their destruction. Does that mean that our tragic flaw will ultimately lead to our undoing? Not at all. Jesus offered the simple solution to the disciples in Gethsemane: "Watch and pray."

"Watch" means "be alert and aware, know yourself, and be on guard lest your momentum take you over the cliff." The first step, then, is to *become aware* of our own tragic flaw, which is ordinarily just the shadow side or the excess of our strengths. The virtues of taking hold which we studied and sought to practice in the first part should have given us at least initial insight into these tendencies.

At the heart of this overconfidence is really a false image of self. We have made our strength our god. And when we find ourselves in this state it is wonderful to have a loved one or close friend who can see deeper into us than we can see into ourselves. My mother was like that. Although she was always very affirming, she could see through my vanities and call me down to earth. Because I knew she loved me, it didn't hurt so much. That's what Mary means to me now as my spiritual mother. She enables me to laugh at myself when my balloon bursts and I land back in the real world. I have especially come to appreciate it when, before I crash, she shows me how I have exaggerated something and gently leads me to tame my unbridled impetuosity.

Meditations

Reflect on the example of Peter, who was unaware of his tendencies and even denied them. See also these Scriptures: 1

Corinthians 4:7; Galatians 6:3; Matthew 6:1,4; Romans 7:22-23.

Exercises

- Take some quiet time and ask yourself what your strong points are, the things you find it easiest to do, or that you feel most eager to do. What are the traits for which others often praise you? A personality inventory might be helpful in this regard. Have you let these tendencies run your life to an extreme at times? What do you need to balance these tendencies?

- Read *The Seven Miracles of Gubbio and the Eighth* by R.L. Bruckberger (New York: Whittlesey House, 1948). This simple allegory based on a legend from the life of St. Francis shows how the wolf's strong point became his undoing.

- Practice giving praise to God for the strengths and gifts you have instead of taking pride in yourself. Then ask his help in becoming aware of those areas in your life which need changing.

- Ask Mary to help you identify your needs and then learn from her how to trust God. Reflect on some specific examples in your life when you found that trusting in God helped you to overcome some circumstance where you would have failed had you tried on your own, even though you thought your strength sufficient to the challenge.

Steps on the Journey

1. What strengths do people usually recognize in you?

2. To what excesses do these strengths sometimes invite you?

3. Would you care to relate an experience where one of your strengths led you to go too far?

4. Have you found Mary a helpful influence in taming your strengths?

Lord Jesus, I want to follow you. I thank you for the strengths that you have given me, but I ask that I may ever remember they are your gifts. Keep me from following them blindly, lest I fall as Peter did. Mother Mary, may the thought of you bring gentle but perceptive discernment to the movements of my heart and soul, that God may be glorified in all things. Amen.

SEVENTEEN

Knowing What God Wants

W HEN I WAS TWELVE YEARS OLD, my father took my brothers and me on a late afternoon deer hunt in one of the distant pastures of our ranch, which is situated in the Texas hill country. He dropped me off with instructions on how to reconnect with the rest of the party after sundown. I was to reach a certain fence, cross it, turn left, and work my way down a hill. They would meet me at the foot of that hill. It all sounded foolproof.

When darkness fell, I had not found the fence. I was lost, without even moonlight to guide my steps. Which way should I turn? I remember panicking, walking faster, scaring a deer (which scared me), until I heard the distant call of my father's voice and soon spotted his car's headlights.

Being lost is an unsettling experience, even in something as simple as not finding a certain street in an unknown part of a city. In the spiritual life, too, we sometimes feel lost. We're not sure what to do. We don't know which decision is the right one, or the better one. We can usually identify choices that would be evil, but among the many *good* choices before us, which is the best?

A ROAD MAP FOR THE JOURNEY

Little choices face us every day; most are made with relative ease. But occasionally indecision stops us cold. If we spend much time worrying about what we should do, we waste a lot of energy and peace of soul. Scrupulosity is an extreme form of wasted energy, but we often bump up against less formidable barriers to action. On the other hand, we may plunge into one direction or undertake a project only to find that our efforts were ill conceived. In retrospect, it didn't seem to be part of God's plan. Again, we have wasted time and energy.

What can we do in the grip of indecision or in the aftermath of impetuosity? The same thing we do when we can't find the street we're looking for: ask for help.

For the Christian, the helper is first of all the Holy Spirit. The help he gives in our decision-making is called the gift of discernment. St. Paul speaks of this gift in his letter to the Philippians: "This is what I pray for: that your love may abound more and more in knowledge and discernment for every instance, so that you may discover what is really important, enabling you to be pure and blameless for the day of Christ, to the glory and praise of God" (Phil 1:9-11).

The expression "perception to discern what is of value" can also be translated: "discernment for every instance, that you may be able to distinguish real values." In the moral order, this gift is not unlike one used in the physical order by mohair sorters. I have watched seasoned veterans take a handful of angora goat hair and by a deft touch assess not only the length of the hair but even its breadth. Then they make an instantaneous judgment as to which of some twenty categories the hair belongs—based on a single touch.

When I later learned about the Holy Spirit's gift of discernment, the trade of mohair sorting helped me to understand it. The Holy Spirit gives us the skill to gracefully and quickly make judgments which are most in tune with the will of God.

To receive this direction, prayer must be our first recourse before making any important decision. We also need simplicity and purity of intention, openness of heart to what God wants (not telling him ahead of time what he must say), and trust in God. He seldom responds by means of a heavenly voice; it more often comes as a gentle nudge or a spiritual attraction which may go against our natural tendencies.

Mary means many things to me, but it is in her role as counselor that I treasure her most. Lady Wisdom in the Old Testament was the counselor of kings and commoners alike. For me Mary is this counselor. She is a kind of visible instrument of the Holy Spirit, concretizing his inner movements for me in ways that are humanly understandable. I find great peace and strength in sifting alternatives in the presence of Mary. She just seems to take the anxiety out of decision-making. Discernment, after all, is not merely a matter of counting up the pros and cons. It is a matter of weighing them, and that means a matter of the heart as well as the mind.

But in God's plan, in addition to ministry of the Holy Spirit and Mary, many of his graces are ministered to us through fellow pilgrims in our daily lives. At times we need to seek the counsel of a trusted friend, spouse, parent, spiritual director, confessor, or superior. Such a consultation is not an abdication of responsibility; it is rather a legitimate way of attaining greater clarity and certainty before moving ahead with a decision.

We can also pursue more general sources that offer practical wisdom: reading, study, inspirational movies, videos, or audiotapes. The more enlightened our mind, the brighter will be the light in which we make daily decisions.

Meditations

God is the source of all wisdom, and it may be had for the asking (Wis 6:12; Jas 1:5). Jesus is the light of the world, the light by which to walk (Jn 8:12; Ps 36:10). The Holy Spirit will teach us what we need to know (Jn 14:26). "Try to discover what the Lord wants of you" (Eph 5:10). Neglecting counsel deprives us of much of God's direction in our lives (Eccl 4:10; Jn 12:35). The Lord gives us guides (Acts 9:8; Lk 10:16).

Exercises

- The next time you're faced with a decision, take the matter first to prayer. Ask the Lord to purify your heart, to remove selfish passion, and to put you in his peace. Then list the reasons for and against the alternatives at hand. Such reasons are not so much to be numbered as to be weighed. Circle the ones that weigh heaviest. Ask Mary to help you make the decision in the light of the Holy Spirit. If the decision is an important one, have recourse to counsel.

- Our modern culture does not encourage us to make choices based on Christian values (think of the reasons we are often given for buying a product). If you had to create a goodwill advertisement aimed at helping people make a Christian decision about a crucial matter in their lives, how would you do it?

- What strategies will you follow in the future when you have an important decision to make?

Steps on the Journey

1. What has been your usual process for decision-making? Has prayer been part of it? What about consultation with others?

2. How could you improve your decision-making? Would it help for Mary to be a part of it?

3. Do you feel better before or after making a decision? If before, then you may tend to put off decisions too much. If after, you may tend to make decisions too quickly, without weighing all the evidence.

4. How does good discernment lead you to a deeper union with God?

Father, I praise you for supplying my every need. Your Holy Spirit inspires me and offers me the gift of discernment. And you have made available to me others to whom I may turn for counsel in my hesitations. Keep me from the pride of not asking directions even when I know I'm lost. Mary, when I gaze upon your peaceful countenance, I find there the assurance that the Lord will be with me in every detail of my life and that he will show me the way, even as he did with you. Amen.

EIGHTEEN

Meeting Opposition

I N ONE SENSE, interior strength should keep exterior obstacles from throwing us off course. Yet we often meet obstacles which get the best of us, sometimes because they carry an element of surprise. After all, we can become familiar with our weaknesses and strengths and hesitations, but external events can exert pressures for which we are unprepared. We need to be aware that "surprise attacks" can occur at any moment and, as much as possible with God's grace, we need to be ready for them.

SHOULD WE FIGHT, FLEE, OR FLOW?

One kind of surprise attack takes the form of opposition. If we were involved in criminal activity of some kind, we would expect to run up against the law or meet resistance from someone we had harmed. But the surprise comes when we encounter opposition or persecution while doing good.

Sometimes the opposition comes from an individual or group whose selfish interests are threatened by our actions. Jesus faced continued resistance from the established religious powers of his day, as did St. Thomas More and many of the martyrs. A Marianist priest, Fr. Jakob Gapp, continued to speak out against Hitler. He was imprisoned in Berlin's Plötzenzee prison and later beheaded. But sometimes the opposition comes from people whose support we expected. And most painfully, the opposition sometimes comes from members of our own families, communities, or workplaces.

How should we respond to such opposition? Our choices are basically to *fight*, to *flee*, or to *flow*. An aggressive response is likely to increase the opposition and move it from a disagreement on issues to a conflict of persons. Fighting can also divert creative energy from whatever good we are doing and thus diminish our productivity.

In choosing not to fight, we could instead choose to flee. Doing so would mean giving up the good work and the dream. In the face of criticism, rejection, backbiting, insidious criticism of insiders, or blatant opposition of outsiders, we can begin to get worn down. We can say, "Who needs this?" and quit. We forget that the works of God come with a price tag. The redemption of the world cost Jesus his life. The redemption of our little corner of the world bears a price tag as well: our own share in the cross.

The best way to handle opposition is to flow. We can embrace the promise of Jesus that if they persecuted him they will persecute his disciples too (Jn 15:18-25). We can hold on to the dream and accept, even welcome, persecution because it conforms us to Jesus. "The apostles left the Sanhedrin, rejoicing that they had been deemed worthy to suffer disgrace for the name [of Jesus]" (Acts 5:41).

I remember seeing a special joy on the faces of brothers and sisters in Nepal who had been arrested, beaten, and jailed because of their Christian faith. All my life I had lived in a country that was at least nominally Christian, where being a priest carried a certain honor. But at that time, I was living in a country where the Christian faith was really not welcomed.

Knowing the persecution my friends were suffering, I became depressed. And, although I was not in jail, I felt at one with those who were because of their faith. As I huddled under a heavy emotional cloud, I remembered the word of Jesus, "Pray for your persecutors" (Mt 5:44). And as soon as I began to pray for them, the cloud suddenly lifted and I felt myself raised above the circumstances. I was graced with Jesus' own victory.

Our spiritual journey is reaching a new plateau. The patience we sought to practice in the preparation virtues (mastering the circumstances) is being moved by God to a new register. We are beginning to take on the patience of God. When in difficulties we do what we can and then leave the outcome to God. The fruit is deep peace, even joy.

Fr. Chaminade said of himself, "I am a brook that, faced with an obstacle, merely grows deeper till it flows over it." May we also learn to flow with the grace of God until we overflow the banks of opposition.

Nowadays the poor and those who work with them frequently face incredible odds in trying to improve their situation. They could simply crumble under it, which is exactly what their opponents would like them to do. But many of them are learning to stand tall, aware of their dignity as children of God, uniting their forces and claiming justice. In so doing they are joining Mary in her magnificat, where she glorifies the God who champions the cause of the poor and the downtrodden: "He puts down the proud and raises the lowly." She too was one of those poor. She was sought out by Herod, who wanted to kill her Son. No one would welcome her in Bethlehem. And she so identified with Jesus that opposition to him was also opposition to her. At the final consummation, at the cross, the evangelist describes her role in one word: she *stood*. She was the strong woman.

From her and with her we can learn to "hang in there," faithfully continuing to do the work the Lord has given us, even if it leads us, like her, to Calvary. The consolation she promises: we are in good company and await with confidence our hope of glory!

Meditations

Reflect on the patient endurance of Jesus (1 Pt 2:21; 4:1) and of Mary (Mt 2:13-18; Jn 19:25-27). Consider the lot of the disciple (2 Tm 3:12; Mt 5:10; Mk 10:30). Patience enables us to rejoice in the midst of opposition (Col 1:11-12; 1 Pt 4:13-14; Acts 5:41).

Exercises

- After prayer and meditation, ask the Lord to reveal to you those situations which make you respond with either aggression or flight. Ask the grace to reimage yourself. Trusting in the power of God's grace, try to foresee some situation in which you will react differently.

- Reflect on one or two recent situations when some good work of yours met with opposition from persons from whom you most expected support. Perhaps you presented a good idea to your colleagues, who ridiculed you or told you it just wouldn't work. How did you feel and what was your reaction? How could putting this virtue into practice help you overcome the temptation to fight inappropriately, or to give up trying to improve the situation?

- Think of instances in Mary's life that can help you learn how to live this virtue. Imagine her fear when the people closest to Jesus deserted him, at the persecution by Herod, at the betrayal by Judas. How can her responses to opposition help in handling situations in your daily life? In this connection I cannot recommend too strongly two books by Peter Daino, S.M., coming out of his experience with poor women in Africa who reflect Mary's strength: *Stabat Mater: Noble Icon of the Outcast and the Poor* (Staten Island: Alba House, 1988) and *Mary, Mother of Sorrow, Mother of Defiance* (Maryknoll: Orbis, 1993).

Steps on the Journey

1. Have you been tempted to give up some good work or cause because of opposition? What was your reaction?

2. If someone came to you and complained about opposition to a good work he or she was doing, what would be your response?

3. What kinds of deeper motives is God trying to purify in you when you run into opposition?

4. How can Mary lead you to a deeper union with Jesus in the mystery of perseverance under opposition?

Lord Jesus, when I am faced with opposition for doing good, be my shield and defender. Give me the inner strength not to crumble or withdraw. Teach me how to respond rather than react. May I learn from your mother how to stand beneath your cross. Give me the enduring patience that will ultimately claim the victory. Amen.

NINETEEN

Facing Seductions

A RELIGIOUS I KNOW was making a thirty-day Ignatian retreat. At one point when he was lying prostrate before the tabernacle and praying intensely, he suddenly heard an inner voice saying: *Leave religious life*. This man was greatly disturbed and broke out into a sweat. Because it brought disturbance instead of peace, the fruit of the Spirit (Gal 5:22), his retreat director later reassured him that such a suggestion would hardly have been from the Lord.

While attacks of this magnitude may be less frequent, we are daily assaulted by lesser spirits, most often perhaps by the spirit of excuses: "I'm too old for that" (like Abraham); "I'm too young for that" (like Jeremiah); "I need my rest"; "Fasting would injure my health"; "I deserve a break"—and so on. The appeal from such excuses comes from the fact that they're often based on partial truths; their insidiousness comes from the fact that they're often not true or not entirely true.

Many of us use excuses as a defensive weapon against the courage it takes to follow the Lord in a given situation. While proposing to appeal to common sense, suggestions of this type really play on our fears of change, risk, and sacrifice. So we remain stuck in our spiritual journey, while the Lord is calling us to move ahead with him. We either abandon a work or trim our expectations and our efforts to fit our own comfortable dimensions. Thus, we fall short of the good we could do for the glory of God.

WHAT'S THE REMEDY?

Paul spells out the remedy: "[B]e transformed by the renewal of your mind, that you may discern what is the will of God, what is good and pleasing and perfect" (Rom 12:2, NAB). We need to feed our mind daily and generously on the Word of God. We need to set aside time for retreat and reflection to periodically refocus our priorities. We need to listen in prayer to the suggestions of the Holy Spirit, remembering that God knows that by his grace we are capable of much more than we can imagine (Eph 3:20).

Some years ago I had an operation on my knee. The morning after the operation the doctor came in and told me to lift my leg. Looking at him as if he were insane, I told him I couldn't.

"Yes, you can," he said. So I tried and couldn't—I was *sure* I couldn't.

"Lift your leg," the doctor insisted.

After a few more rounds of debate, I finally got tired of arguing and lifted my leg! The doctor knew I could do something I just *knew* I couldn't do! Doctor Jesus sometimes counters our excuses with his divine knowledge: "You can!"

Ever since the people of God came into the land of the Canaanites, they have been vulnerable to the seductions of the surrounding cultures. The Canaanites had a very sensual worship; they often offered their firstborn in human sacrifice and engaged in prostitution as part of their sacred rites. Later the Christians had to face a culture in which the pagans exposed children to death, molested their slaves, and indulged their appetites in sensuous theaters and orgies.

Is our post-Christian culture much different? Advertisers tell us what is "chic" to wear, how we should look, what we *must* have to be popular. Television shows depict fornication and adultery as normal fare, and violence on the screen escalates. Surveys show that the media give better coverage to the "pro-choice" side of the abortion debate than to the pro-life side. People are told that condoms assure safe sex, when a 16 percent failure rate has been documented.

In Roman times Christians used to be able to shut their doors and avoid the theaters, but now one never knows what's coming next on the TV screen in the living room. Even simplistic one-liners pass on values, like the one I heard the other day, "Beauty, like morality, is in the eye of the beholder." The implication is that morality is totally subjective.

Seduction is a type of temptation that appeals to our mind, not merely to our senses. It presents falsehood under the guise of truth and good. For that reason it can appeal to the most spiritual motives in us. When the devil saw that he could not succeed in tempting Jesus to satisfy his physical hunger, he tried another ploy. He took him to the pinnacle of the temple and invited him to jump off. This would prove the truth of Scripture that the angels would take care of him (Mt 4:5-6). In our lives, too, we can sometimes be seduced by apparently spiritual values.

Today the New Age movement is seducing many who are in search of truth, good, and happiness. There are other philosophies abroad as well which appear to offer the truth but are not in accord with the truth of Jesus Christ. Even some degreed theologians are promoting teachings contrary to those of the church. In times of confusion, we find clarity in clinging to the church, which is the pillar and mainstay of the truth (1 Tm 3:15), and to its teaching authority.

Besides immersing ourselves in the Word of God as it is handed on to us in the church, what else can we do to remain faithful to the Lord and to our covenants? One of the best ways is to frequently renew our commitments—whether to our baptismal promises or marriage or religious vows. We can easily take for granted that the promises we made years ago maintain their vigor as we pass through new and more difficult terrain in our spiritual journey.

The sad experience of others who have failed assures us that perseverance is not a grace upon which we can presume. The last petition of the Lord's Prayer sums up our need: that we not be put to a testing beyond our strength. Frequent, even daily, renewal of our commitments enables us to cooperate with the grace of fidelity, which is ours for the asking.

For those who have made a consecration to Mary, the daily renewal of *Totus tuus* can be a powerful bulwark against the untruths or half-truths that would deter us from faithfully following the Lord. After all, Mary is the New Eve. The Eve of Genesis was seduced by the serpent, who told her not only that nothing would happen if she disobeyed the Lord, but that she would even come to know as God knows. She listened (her first mistake), then noticed that the fruit was tasty, beautiful, and desirable for the wisdom it would give. Mary listened too, but she listened to God and obeyed his wishes. In so doing she ushered in the incarnation of the Son of God and the whole redemptive mystery that followed.

Mary stands on the head of the serpent, symbol of God's total conquest of evil and sin in her. Now, in her glorified state, she is the woman in whose presence Michael the archangel defeats the dragon. Satan cannot fool God, nor can he fool his Christ and the woman in whom the grace of Christ was totally victorious. For that reason, Mary is an excellent armor against the seductions of the world, the devil, and our own sin-prone tendencies.

But why does God allow us to experience seductions? They can be a "wake-up" call to us to ground ourselves more deeply in prayer, in the Word of God, and in our commitment to Jesus. In this way they purify us of our assumptions that we don't have to "watch" or "remain awake" spiritually. They can be the occasions of moving us to a greater trust in God.

Meditations

Reflect on Jesus' agony in the garden, when he could have abandoned the way of the cross but found his peace in surrender to the Father's will. If you are a disciple, when you put your hand to the plow, you will not look back (Lk 9:62). Hold firm, do not lose your prize (Rv 3:11). Renew your baptismal promises, renouncing Satan and claiming Jesus as your Lord and Savior.

Exercises

- In a time of reflective prayer, think of situations where you may have decided to abandon a good work. What were your reasons? Was your decision based on reading the signs of God's will, or were you giving in to fear and cowardice, or trimming the sails of your dreams because they asked too much of you? Ask Mary to be with you as a gentle counselor. Pray that in all future endeavors you will follow God's call—even if it means the rough road, the narrow gate, or the cross.

- Modern culture bombards us with messages such as seeking personal fulfillment in all that we do or putting our needs first (take that drink, smoke that cigarette, don't forgive those who offend you until they apologize first). We can overcome this type of thinking by remembering that our first commitment is to God's plan for our lives. Reflect on how a commitment to his plan requires daily reminders. How can you begin to build into your daily routine a renewal of your commitment to God? Take a few moments each morning and each evening to renew your commitment to Jesus Christ.

- Prayerfully reflect on your commitments as a Christian (your baptismal vows and any marriage or religious or private vows). If you have made a personal consecration to Mary, include reflection on what this means to you.

- Read C.S. Lewis' *The Screwtape Letters* (Urichsville, Ohio: Barbour, 1992) to gain an insight into how diabolical seduction works.

Steps on the Journey

1. To what seductions of your surrounding culture do you find yourself especially vulnerable?

2. Think of friends or loved ones who fell prey to some seduction of the culture. How could they have avoided it?

3. What means have you taken in the past to avoid the seductions of the surrounding culture?

4. How do you understand the role of Mary in overcoming seductions?

Father, with Jesus I pray for the grace of fidelity. In a world of shattered dreams and broken promises, this is no small grace. Let it be your voice that I always hear, not the voices even of good people who would dissuade me from your call in my life. Mary, you were blessed because you heard the Word of God and kept it. Give me your listening heart. Amen.

Trials and
Temptations

ONE OF THE MOST PURIFYING EXPERIENCES in the spiritual life is, strangely enough, temptation. It is a word not heard much in modern spirituality, but it certainly is biblical. Abraham was put to the test in the sacrifice of Isaac (Gn 22). Job was tested by a landslide of woes and tempted by his wife to curse God. God told Cain that sin was crouching at his door (Gn 4:7). Jesus was tempted in the desert by the devil and during his ministry by his enemies. Even Peter merited the title "Satan" in trying to block Jesus from the cross.

Sometimes the tempter wins, as he did in Judas' betrayal of Jesus and momentarily in Peter's denial. When we win, with God's grace, we come out stronger—especially if we counter the temptation with an opposing act of virtue. From the Gospel story of Jesus' temptation we learn an important lesson: to use the Word of God as a sword to vanquish the enemy.

It may seem at first sight that there is little difference between temptations and the seductions we discussed in the preceding chapter. It is true that seduction is a form of temptation. There is a slight difference, however, in that seductions appeal more to the mind through deception, whereas other temptations have a strong pull on the will and the emotions even when we know we are being tempted to do something clearly wrong.

With sexual temptations, the traditional advice is to flee— that is, not to argue or hesitate but to leave the situation or the thought or the image by immediately turning to something else. In this case, the maxim often proves true that the one who hesitates is lost.

With other temptations the conventional wisdom has been to stand and fight: "Resist the devil, and he will flee from you" (Jas 4:7, NAB). "Be sober and vigilant. Your opponent the devil is prowling around like a roaring lion looking for [someone] to devour. Resist him, steadfast in faith" (1 Pt 5:8-9, NAB).

Each stage of human life is prone to particular temptations. In childhood, it might be to disobedience, lying to one's parents, or fighting with one's brothers or sisters. The teenage urge for independence and the onset of puberty present even more possibilities for temptations, but also the challenge of responsibility for one's decisions. Beginning one's career brings further challenges, as we encounter others in the workplace who are willing to cut corners or to climb over others to get to the top. We begin to wonder why we shouldn't do the same. Then there is the famous middle-age crisis, when one realizes that life is half over with most of one's youthful dreams unrealized. Boredom or depression may set in and invite one to extramarital affairs or the possibility of underhanded professional gain. Retirement and aging bring still other temptations: to become a grouch, to complain of one's aches and pains, to blame others for our unfulfilled dreams, or maybe even to ask, "Is this all there is?" Imminent death presents another kind of challenge as we choose in our final acts what seal we will give to our life.

Perhaps the greatest temptation I have faced in my religious life has been the temptation to cling to securities when God is obviously calling me to let go and move on. I don't like risk. In high school I dropped out of football after a couple of days' practice because it demanded too great a change in me. Thank

God, when I entered the Marianists, I had no choice whether to play soccer or not. And one Sunday we did it in the mud four different times! I learned a lot by being forced to do something I detested. It helped shape my character in ways that I would never have chosen.

Now that I am older I have more choice in the risks I take, but for that very reason I have to beware of the temptation of security. Jesus and Mary are constantly inviting me to take risks, and I don't like it any more than I did the first soccer game I had to play—but that's the way I grow.

Describing Christian combat in terms of the armor and equipment of a Roman soldier, Paul stresses that our warfare is not against human beings but against the spiritual powers of evil:

> Draw your strength from the Lord and from his mighty power. Put on the armor of God so that you may be able to stand firm against the tactics of the devil. For our struggle is not with flesh and blood but with the principalities, with the powers, with the world rulers of this present darkness, with the evil spirits in the heavens. Therefore, put on the armor of God, that you may be able to resist on the evil day and, having done everything, to hold your ground. So stand fast with your loins girded in truth, clothed with righteousness as a breastplate, and your feet shod in readiness for the gospel of peace. In all circumstances, hold faith as a shield, to quench all [the] flaming arrows of the evil one. And take the helmet of salvation and the sword of the Spirit, which is the word of God. **Ephesians 6:10-17**

God does not want us to live in perpetual spiritual paranoia, fearful of the devil's constant pursuit. It is not mature spirituality to give the devil more attention than he deserves. For Jesus has conquered: "The prince of this world is cast out" (Jn 12:31). On the other hand, neither is it mature spirituality to live as if we were totally immune to temptation or to demonic influence. Periodic crises in our journey should convince us that we need to call on God's help and the power of his Word.

As mentioned earlier, Mary is often depicted crushing the head of the Serpent. The imagery comes from Genesis 3:15, where the history of the human race is presented as a struggle of the Woman and her Son against the power of the Serpent. The Serpent hasn't a chance, for in God's counsel he is already defeated. But, in the apocalyptic imagery of Revelation 12, the Serpent is cast down to earth, where he continues his attack on "the other children" of the Woman.

The fight isn't over. And the Woman has not abandoned her other children who are still traveling the way. Mary promises to aid us in the fight. We just need to remember that there's a war on.

Meditations

Jesus gives us a model in dealing with temptation (Mt 4:1-11; Lk 4:1-13). Those who serve the Lord must be ready for trials (Sir 2:1). Scripture tells us to be on our guard against temptation, to pray and resist (Mt 6:13; 26:41; Jas 4:7; 1 Pt 5:8). God's grace is always available in sufficient measure (1 Cor 10:13; 2 Cor 12:9). We have the temptation of Eve and Adam (Gn 3) versus Mary and the conquest of Satan (Rv 12).

Exercises

- In prayer, review the strategies and tactics you've used in past moments of temptation. Did they work? How could you have done better? What did you learn?

- Reflect on more recent trials. What helped you to overcome—a sense of God's presence, an awareness of Mary's protection, a renewal of your vows, a renewal of your desire to follow Jesus?

- What insights can you gain from the earlier virtues (for example, silence of words, inner silence, mastering the circumstances) regarding specific actions you can take when facing temptation?

Steps on the Journey

1. What temptations are you most vulnerable to? (Remember that these will often be simply to take some good thing or some personal strength to excess.)

2. Have you found recourse to Mary helpful in the past?

3. Are there particular temptations that come with certain periods in life? What period are you at now, and what might be the particular temptation that might strike you at your age?

Lord Jesus, you taught us to pray, "Lead us not into temptation," that is, "Do not let us fall when tested." I know that I've been tempted in the past and that temptations and trials lie on the path ahead. Give me the strength to identify an invitation as a temptation, a test of my fidelity. And give me the grace to dismiss the tempter, as you did, with the power of God's Word. Mary, Immaculate Victress over the demon, be ever at my side, and let not the enemy claim what belongs to you. Amen.

Part Four

❦

Letting God

Letting God

This stage can be called the stage of *consummation*. Actually, the highest virtues of the Christian life are *faith, hope, and love.* During the first two stages of growth, the Holy Spirit was working in us through these virtues, even though the terrain was much more earthly. In the preparation virtues, we learned to take responsibility for our lives. In the stage of purification, we learned to let the Lord deal with the roots of our old life by our letting go and trusting him. It was our faith in Jesus and our trust in him, aided by docility to Mary, that inspired our journey. And obviously the end and crowning of all our striving is love—purer, stronger love of the Lord and of our neighbor. The apparent complexity of the earlier work came not from God's side but from ours. We wanted God to take over all the dimensions of our lives. So with Mary we looked at those different dimensions.

Consummation, then, means living totally by faith, hope, and love. In a sense the virtues of consummation can be compared to the flight of an airplane when it reaches its cruising altitude. Until then it is climbing, burning a lot of fuel, and often passing through turbulence. At the cruising altitude the ride is smoother, less fuel is wasted, the cabin is quieter. Similarly, in the first two stages faith, hope, and love were manifested in our struggles to get control of ourselves, to negotiate the turbulence in our lives, to gradually turn the controls over to the Lord. In the stage of consummation, there is greater inner quiet and the journey seems to require less effort on our part since God is more and more taking over. It is not that we have nothing more to do. It means that our energies are now available to the Lord and to the kingdom. We can do great things for God because we are not weighed down by the little preoccupations and distractions that wasted so much of our energies earlier.

At each stage there is a "human face" to faith, hope, and love. As Lady Wisdom in the Old Testament instructed her children in very practical habits of living, so Mary instructed us in some very practical behaviors. In the first stage she taught us how to "take hold" of our lives, in the second to "let go." All the while, faith, hope, and love were active, but the human face of growing at that time was very practical and down to earth. She showed us what we needed to do to become docile to the Holy Spirit at each of these earlier stages. There is a human face in the consummation stage too. What does the disciple of Jesus, the child of Mary, look like in this ultimate stage? What enfleshment do faith, hope, and love take on here?

Fr. Chaminade described them in a surprisingly lowly way: they are humility, modesty, self-denial, and renunciation of the world. At first sight these look more like beginners' virtues, and indeed we need them in some measure at every stage. But here, as we shall see, it is the *consummate mode* of these virtues that is at issue. They are the transparencies through which faith, hope, and love shine through in our lives. They are thus a way not merely of letting go, but of *letting God*. This was the way Jesus and Mary let God shine through in a brilliant, unobstructed way. It is also the mark of the saints and holy men and women on the way.

Indeed, at this stage the Lord is finally having his way with us. We no longer hinder what he is trying to do in the world. We are totally at his service and the service of the kingdom, as were Jesus and Mary. People who reach this stage will usually be involved in great projects for the kingdom of God. However deeply personal these virtues seem to be, they make us more available to God for his work on earth. In short, we are *consumed* by the fire of God's love.

Ideally, we experience this consummation without self-consciousness. We are not so much aware of practicing virtues as of being united with Jesus and Mary. Rather than attached to virtue as our own, we feel bonded to the Lord in an other-centered way and become available to others with a new freedom.

We can approach the virtues of consummation in two different ways. One is to study them, to admire them, even to aspire to them. The other is to experience them, to be called by God and drawn into them because of the virtues of preparation and the purification of the Holy Spirit.

Anyone can benefit from the first way. The second way depends on our inner readiness, on the fruitfulness of our preceding work, and most of all on the moment of God's grace. As with all spiritual growth, entering into these virtues of consummation is more a matter of responding to a call from God than of our own efforts.

All the more important, then, is the preceding work of preparation and purification. They have prepared us to hear that call. Professional mountain climbers do not fly in to base camp one day and begin climbing Mount Everest the next. They spend two weeks trekking from the capital city of Kathmandu, climbing through the foothills, getting adjusted to the higher altitudes, and toning up their bodies to prepare for the rigors of the climb.

Similarly, we might look at the consummation virtues from afar and aspire to the ascent. But we would do well to make sure we are in peak condition before expecting that we can really manage them. In fact, after studying these virtues, we usually find it necessary to review and deepen our work by returning to the previous stages.

TWENTY-ONE

All Is Gift

H UMILITY, THE SUBJECT OF THIS CHAPTER, is probably the
most misunderstood of all the virtues. The popular view
is that it is practiced by people who have a poor self-image and
are always putting themselves down. In fact, such behavior is
usually a cry for others to affirm them. But we also live in the
wake of Muhammad Ali and other stars who claim, "I'm the
greatest." And advertisers try to make us think that their product is actually the very best on the market. They quote only
those surveys that put them on top. Can you imagine an ad
saying, "Our product isn't the best, but we think you'll be satisfied with it." They would never say that even if it's true.

But we do find something irresistible in a person like
Mother Teresa, who seems never to have a thought for herself,
so consumed is she for the plight of the poorest of the poor.
She would not deny the good that she has done for the poor,
nor the good done by her religious. Instead, she would probably praise God for what he has done in and through her and
say, "But this is only a drop in the ocean of the world's misery.
There is so much yet to be done!" And that, of course, would
be true. Humility, St. Teresa of Avila said long ago, is truth.
Humility is the clear glass that lets God shine through.

Humility is something that can hardly be worked at directly.
Fr. Chaminade even said, "It's an illusion to work at humility

too early." That's why it comes at the end rather than at the beginning of the journey. For humility is the total emptiness of self that comes from being filled with God. We don't empty a glass of air before pouring in the water. The water expels the air automatically.

Well, then, is there anything to be done at all at this stage? Yes, for precisely because we have arrived at a certain amount of virtue and have probably by now accomplished some important things for God, a secret complacency can set in. We can even think, in our unguarded moments, how fortunate God is to have instruments like us at his disposal!

This is the stage where the first beatitude becomes real: "Blessed are the poor in spirit." It is poverty of spirit, the realization that God is all, and that all we have is gift, pure gift. Even our capacity to receive is God's gift. And so in this state we live in a constant attitude of thanksgiving.

Especially do we shun flattery, either of ourselves or others. When due praise does come our way, we realize, "What have we that we have not received?" (see 1 Cor 4:7). One of my Marianist brothers once told me, "Whenever I receive a compliment, there are a thousand people who should take a bow." And ultimately all comes from God himself.

Jesus lived this attitude perfectly and it attracted others: "Come to me... for I am meek and humble of heart" (Mt 11:28-29). Fr. Chaminade comments: "We who have the grace and the revelation of Jesus Christ, who have been born again by the blood of this divine Savior... should attribute nothing to ourselves because all is in God and comes from God. We should seek to eliminate from our heart the slightest return to self, any movement to put ourselves in the place of the author of all good and take complacency in it—that is idolatry, even though it be transitory, light, almost imperceptible."[1]

The humility at issue here is more a gift of God than the fruit of our efforts, more something to be sought and prayed for than to be worked at. Fr. Jacques Olier, the seventeenth-century founder of the Sulpicians, described this kind of state:

"Perfect purity of soul cleansed of all pride makes the soul desire nothing, wish nothing, believe itself nothing, act in nothing by itself. What then must happen? God must possess the soul and work in it according to his good pleasure, and not that the soul should wish to possess God to dispose of him according to its own will."[2]

A soul thus consumed by the love of God is only minimally conscious of itself. The Beloved lives in the lover in such a way that the lover's self-interest seems to disappear. The attention, the applause, the offers of power and prestige that once seemed so important now fade away, and one wishes that all be given to the Beloved. The rejection, humiliation, and persecution once so feared become even sweet. They unite us more deeply with the Beloved who endured such things and convince us that the Beloved alone is all.

True humility is not a put-down of self nor a denial of the gifts God has given us, even of the good we may have done by God's grace. In boasting of God's magnificent works in her, Mary magnified the Lord, not herself. It was part of her very humility that she could say, "The Lord has done great things for me," for she was proclaiming that all was gift. And the gifts were great. She was telling the truth, the whole truth by proclaiming the source of the gifts. This same kind of humility led her, in forgetfulness of self, to see to the needs of others, as she did in serving her cousin Elizabeth and then at Cana upon noticing the wine had run out.

This transparency, this emptiness of self, helps build community and empowers mission. In this state, the ego does not impede the flow of gifts and ministries, for it does not seek status or even praise but is happy to give it to others and ultimately to God.

Meditations

Reflect on the self-emptying of Jesus (Phil 2:6-11). We learn humility from him (Mt 11:29). Mary is the humble servant of the Lord (Lk 1:38). She gives all the glory to

God (Lk 1:46-55). God exalts the lowly (Lk 1:51; Jas 4:6; Lk 18:14).

Exercises

- In prayer make a list of the most outstanding talents you have, and then give God the praise and glory.
- Think of some recent project where you accepted full credit for what was accomplished. If others worked with you, did you acknowledge their contributions? Did you give thanks to God for giving you the talents to carry out the responsibilities you had?

Steps on the Journey

1. How did you understand the virtue of humility prior to reading this chapter? How do you understand it now?

2. Is it pride to number your gifts and acknowledge them?

3. How does one arrive at humility without "working at it directly"?

4. Think of someone you consider truly humble. Is this an attractive trait? How do you think they came by it?

5. How was humility expressed in the life of Mary? How can she lead us into the humility of Jesus?

Lord Jesus, let me learn from you what humility of heart really is. May I not deprive you of glory by denying your gifts to me, but let me realize that I have nothing that I have not received, and that to you belongs the glory of the Giver. Mary, teach me to say your Magnificat with my mind and heart totally focused on the Lord, source and giver of all. Amen.

TWENTY-TWO

Living Only for God's Glory

I F THERE IS ANY VIRTUE the modern world despises, it is modesty. Our culture prizes those who are number one, and people who are number one want other people to know. As a youngster I remember being invited to the home of some friends who were entertaining a celebrity. The celebrity talked and talked about herself and her wonderful career without ever asking anybody else in the room who they were, where they came from, and all those usual questions which are normally part of a conversation. She acted as if she were under the floodlights and we were an audience lost in the darkness. Even as a kid, I remembered how bored I was and how bored the rest of my family was. Leaving the house was a liberation.

Most of us would not be as socially gauche as was this celebrity. But there is something in all of us that impels us to be on stage. Think how important some people believe they become when they get on TV, even if it's only for a soundbite. Or think how important it is for some people to be the first to know and the first to tell any bit of news.

If you have a compulsion to be noticed, to be applauded, or to be praised, you have not yet arrived at the consummation virtue of modesty. If you feel depressed or angry when your gifts are overlooked, when you're not called on to serve or shine, when someone seemingly less gifted is promoted or praised—you need to seek the grace of this virtue.

Humility focuses our view of ourselves before God; modesty focuses on how we look before the world. As a consummation virtue, modesty means more than simplicity in dress, grooming, and adornment. How do we handle the gifts God has given us—our natural talents, certainly, but more importantly the gifts of grace that we receive?

How, in other words, do we shepherd and foster the movements of the Holy Spirit so that they are not lost or turned to selfish ends? In particular, how do we behave before others so as to attract them to the Lord rather than to ourselves?

We have all been favored by countless graces, perhaps along with some success in the apostolate, even remarkable success. Are we to hide these graces? Scripture invites us rather to proclaim them to the glory of God: "I will bless the Lord at all times; praise shall be always in my mouth. My soul will glory in the Lord that the poor may hear and be glad.... In my misfortune I called, the Lord heard and saved me from all distress" (Ps 34:2-7).

The psalmist is obviously thinking about specific blessings received from the hand of God. So too in our lives, we give glory to God by witnessing to others what great things he has done for us. Furthermore, gifts of praise, inspired messages, healing, and service are given ultimately to build up the body of Christ (Eph 4:12-16). Paul says such gifts are to be sought (1 Cor 14:1) and used (Rom 12:6-8; 1 Pt 4:10-11).

But as Fr. Tony De Mello has remarked, the ego can feed on anything. Our selfish nature may have been conquered in its lower passions only to reappear in a more spiritual guise later on. The most persistent passion of our ego is to claim things for ourselves, for our own glory and aggrandizement—even the most spiritual things. Paul ran into competitor "apostles" who did just that. To imitate them, he said, would be to make himself a fool. Instead, if he were to boast of anything, it would be of his weaknesses, "that the power of Christ may dwell with me" (2 Cor 12:9).

Humility is its foundation, but modesty specifically aims at glory and praise that come our way. Instead of being an obstacle to the Giver and to the growth of others, our gifts should give glory to God and enable others. At this point the virtue of modesty becomes apostolic. If we are to build the body of Christ, we will use our gifts in a way that enables and encourages others to discover and use *their* gifts to do the same. Rather than operating as a lone ranger, we will delight in working as team members. And we will prefer the common good to our own advantage. What matters is not that we shine but that others be drawn into the kingdom.

In this way we will be cooperating in Mary's power of *attraction*. Lady Wisdom does not overwhelm nor force herself on anyone. She attracts and invites to her banquet (Prv 8:1-9:6). Any disciple formed in the school of Mary should do apostolic works in the same way. Far from being wimpish, modesty enjoys the very attractiveness of divine wisdom and of Mary herself.

I have found this virtue difficult to practice. I have spent my entire professional life in education of one kind or another, either teaching or religious formation. Whenever I'm in charge of a project, I want it to look good. If I do the job myself, I can do it the way "it ought to be done." And I'll look good. But if I delegate portions of the project, thus letting others share the responsibility, I risk a result that may not be as "perfect" as if I had made sure it was done my way. If I can let go of my compulsion to "look good," I can help others grow through service.

Even when I give a homily I think is terrific, I wonder if anyone else thought so. This appetite for having a pat on the back is not quite the same as appreciating an evaluation, good or bad. It messes up the gift aspect of my relationship with others, so that when a compliment does come I receive it more as a payment than a gift.

The "second moment" of good inspirations is also a good check on where we are with this virtue. For example, in prayer I decide to help out at a soup kitchen. *That* was from the Holy Spirit. But, in the next moment, I begin to think how generous and Christlike, even how holy I am. Ugh! "Miserable creature that I am!" (Rom 7:24). Indeed, the ego can feed on anything. Or, as Paul said, even if I give my body to be burned but am not motivated by love, I am nothing (1 Cor 13:2-3). I wonder if I will ever really be where God wants me in growing in this virtue. Maybe my constant awareness of my tendency to possess God's gifts for myself rather than for his glory may at least remind me how much I need him. I do find the company of Mary helpful in turning the glory back to the Lord.

The virtue of modesty also affects our personal prayer. We may at times be visited with extraordinary graces. These gifts should be received with gratitude and should lead us to the Giver, who is obviously more important than his gifts. Unlike children who run away from the Giver to play with the gifts, those who are mature in the spiritual life will instead look all the more intensely into the Giver's eyes to behold the love which gave the gift. Fr. Chaminade, quoting Fr. Jacques Olier, says:

> The soul established in perfect sanctity remains purely united to God by faith... it is detached even from his gifts, since they are not God, who is pure and holy and separated from everything. It is not that we should not use his gifts to go to him, but they must be only the way and we should have no attachment, that we may possess him alone. If we become attached to those things, there is something between us and God which hinders him from uniting himself completely to us.[1]

Our experiences of God touch him but never contain him. When Peter and "the other disciple," whom we take to be

John, ran to the tomb on Easter morning, Peter couldn't make sense of what he saw, even after entering the tomb. But John saw the linen headpiece carefully folded in a place by itself (which wouldn't have been done if the body had been stolen). That sign was sufficient for him to believe that Jesus had risen (Jn 20:4-9). In the same way, we are often given signs of God's presence and action in our lives or in our prayer. They point to, without actually containing, the yet unpossessed. While receiving these divine glimpses with profound gratitude, we must not cling to them as if they were ultimate reality, nor boast of them as chevrons of our holiness, but instead allow them to kindle our thirst for God himself whom we shall one day meet face-to-face.

Modesty was the outstanding virtue of Mary, the most gifted of creatures yet the one most transparent of the Lord, source of all her grandeur. She is told she will be the Messiah's mother; she responds by saying she is just the servant of the Lord. She goes to Elizabeth not to trumpet her own importance but to serve her cousin in need. Except where needed, she remains in the background, for her glory is her Son. Through her we are able to see Jesus, the Father, and the Holy Spirit more clearly than through any other.

Meditations

Not to us but to you be the glory (Ps 115:1). Mary glorifies the Lord (Lk 1:46, 49). The light of the disciples should glorify the Father (Mt 5:16).

Exercises

• Mary is a model of this kind of modesty. If all generations are going to call her blessed, she gives the Lord all the glory for the great things he has done for her. If you want to be effective in bringing God's love to others, think of some ways in which you can practice this virtue. In instances where your ego is hurting (for instance, by being overlooked), thank God because that slight can mean spiritual growth. In what instances are you called upon to put aside your own ego for the good of others?

- Pray for the grace to enjoy remaining in the background and letting others shine. How willing are you to risk having a project turn out a bit sloppy for the sake of giving others a chance to learn?

Steps on the Journey

1. Why do we find braggarts such bores?

2. How does modesty, in the sense described here, become apostolic?

3. How do you respond to praise of your gifts?

4. In what way are God's gifts to us both a means of coming closer to him but also a possible obstacle to deeper union? For example, consider prayer in this light.

5. How can Mary enable us to receive God's gifts fully yet not turn them to selfish ends?

Heavenly Father, you have made us for yourself and our hearts are restless till they rest in you. Show us that the best way to you and to the fullness of life is to hold all your gifts with a relaxed grasp, to let them flow through our hands to others in order that you may fill us more with yourself. Like Mary, let me boast only in the Lord, not in myself nor in the gifts you've given me. May I come to you in the company of her who gave you all the glory for what you accomplished in her. Amen.

TWENTY-THREE

The Cross and the Spirit

THERE COULD HARDLY BE ANYTHING more counter-cultural today than the virtues we are dealing with here. Even the word "virtue" is counter-cultural in a world that emphasizes rights and duties and equality and personal freedom—but virtue? Isn't that terribly Victorian? Isn't self-fulfillment the goal of life?

No. Not according to Jesus. And the "virtue" which he calls his disciples to practice involves the cross. Anyone who wants to be his disciple must take up his cross; anyone who does not cannot be his disciple (Mk 8:34-37). And you gain your life by losing it. Discipleship is costly. It might even mean martyrdom.

In this chapter we take a hard look at this aspect of self-denial, which is another one of those transparent windows through which Jesus himself can be seen. For Jesus was a cross-carrier. And so must we be. But on the other side of the cross is the glory of the resurrection, the gift of the Holy Spirit.

Can we speak of this mystery as a virtue? Fr. Chaminade called it "chaste self-denial." By "self-denial" he simply meant that in the consummate state of discipleship one is so committed to the Lord and the kingdom that selfish interests disappear. By "chaste" he meant the kind of other-centered love that sees the Lord as our spouse and the slightest deviation from him as infidelity to the marriage he has contracted with us.

FLESH AND SPIRIT

Paul spoke about being crucified with Christ (Gal 2:19), but he gives his longest development of this redemptive call when he talks of the struggle between flesh and spirit in Romans 8. Our baptismal consecration, which dealt the death blow to the flesh, initiates a continual struggle against the flesh's remaining tendencies, so that we can be wholly docile to the Holy Spirit:

> For those who live according to the flesh are concerned with the things of the flesh, but those who live according to the spirit with the things of the spirit. The concern of the flesh is death, but the concern of the spirit is life and peace. For the concern of the flesh is hostility toward God; it does not submit to the law of God, nor can it; and those who are in the flesh cannot please God. But you are not in the flesh; on the contrary, you are in the spirit, if only the Spirit of God dwells in you. Whoever does not have the Spirit of Christ does not belong to him. But if Christ is in you, although the body is dead because of sin, the spirit is alive because of righteousness. If the Spirit of the one who raised Jesus from the dead dwells in you, the one who raised Christ from the dead will give life to your mortal bodies also, through his Spirit that dwells in you. Consequently, brothers, we are not debtors to the flesh, to live according to the flesh. For if you live according to the flesh, you will die, but if by the spirit you put to death the deeds of the body, you will live. **Romans 8:5-13, NAB**

Paul again says: "[T]he fruit of the Spirit is love, joy, peace, patience, kindness, generosity, faithfulness, gentleness, self-control.... Now those who belong to Christ [Jesus] have crucified their flesh with its passions and desires. If we live in the spirit, let us also follow the Spirit" (Gal 5:22-25, NAB).

There are thus two dimensions to this virtue of consummation: the negative one, which we can call self-denial or the crucifixion of the "flesh," that is, all self-centered attachments; and the positive one, total docility to the movements of the Holy Spirit.

CUTTING THE THREADS

The first of these dimensions is sometimes called detachment. Now there are three kinds of attachments: those not willed by God, those willed by him, and the "mixed" kind—that is, those attachments God wants us to have but not to hold too tightly. One who is addicted to drugs or alcohol is a victim of attachments that do not bring life; they are certainly not from God. A married man who has an adulterous relationship cannot say that such an attachment is from God. Persons in this situation need a great deal of healing. They need to open themselves to the healing love of God which will set them free.

There are other attachments that God wants us to have: the mutual attachment of husband and wife, parents' attachment to their children, and children's attachment to their parents. When we work with people, if we don't really love them we will not do them much good. And to love means to be attached in a healthy way. For example, we should miss them when we have to leave.

Jesus would not have wept at the death of Lazarus if he had not been lovingly attached to him. When Paul passed through the communities he had founded and told them he would never see them again, they wept. In the sacrament of marriage, each spouse promises "to have and to *hold*" the other. In religious life or the priesthood we should be attached to the community, our students, our parishioners, or the people we serve. These are bonds on which our heavenly Father smiles, because they are bonds created and willed by him.

The problem comes with the third kind of attachments—

the mixed kind. These are attachments which are from God but we hold them *too* tightly. A mother who is so attached to her son that she won't let him leave her to marry and establish a family of his own is possessive and selfish. She has taken a good attachment and ruined it by holding too tightly. A husband or wife who wants every minute of the other's free time is doing the same.

On our ranch, where a family of workers lived, a young boy named Chuey idolized my mother. One hot day he thought he would delight my mother by taking her a banana he had come by. To reach my mother's house, however, he had to travel a mile and a quarter. He did so, clutching the banana tightly in his hot, sweaty hands. When he arrived, he proudly presented his gift to my mother. She, aware of his devotion more than the condition of the gift, accepted it with delight. But the banana was black and mushy because Chuey had held it too tightly. So it can be with good things we hold too tightly.

In the early stages of marriage and in the early stages of religious life, it is important to establish independence of the family of our birth in order to take on the new family to which God has called us. At later stages of life we may become too attached to a place, power, or a position. An extreme example was the man who was not promoted at a university and in reaction took a gun and began shooting the administrators he thought responsible for his being passed over. We can be attached to success, so much so that we are unwilling to risk anything new because it might not succeed—or might not succeed at first. We can be overly attached to persons, if our love for them is possessive rather than liberating.

In short, attaining to this virtue of chaste self-denial is a program for freedom. A bird, St. John of the Cross said, may be held from flight by the tiniest thread. Here we may have to return to some of the discipline we learned in the virtues of preparation. Beyond that, we may fast or do other types of bodily penance, not as a feat of spiritual mountaineering (which would starve the body only to feed the ego), but from a desire to hear God's word more purely and to be sensitive to the slightest whisper of the Holy Spirit.

This work will demand cooperation on our part. But the Lord may also take over the controls as he leads us through the night of the senses and the night of the spirit, of which St. John of the Cross speaks. These are passive purifications with which we simply strive to cooperate, walking by faith and not by sight. In this, the total surrender of the will is more important than the discipline of the body, though the former can hardly be achieved without the latter. The selfish, unredeemed will is also, in Pauline terms, the "flesh," and it too needs to be nailed to the cross. The Lord, who wishes to conquer us by love, is satisfied with nothing short of total surrender.

DOCILITY TO THE HOLY SPIRIT

The second dimension of this virtue is docility to the Holy Spirit. This is the inspiration and goal of the first:

Since *the one who adheres to God is one spirit with him* (1 Cor 6:17), it necessarily follows that the soul well united to God enters into the qualities, the habits, the sentiments and dispositions of God himself, and consequently into the zeal of his justice, which is continual against the flesh. The soul that has entered into God in his zeal and in his holiness, disapproves, condemns, and annihilates in itself all unjust desires which continually rise in his flesh to flatter the senses.[1]

This total availability to the Lord merits being called a spousal relationship. At this consummation stage one begins to experience the reality of Paul's words, "I betrothed you to one husband to present you as a chaste virgin to Christ" (2 Cor 11:2). Or, in the words of Fr. Chaminade, "Spouses of the Holy Spirit live in complete abandonment to his inspiration and holy will." As a spouse keeps all her affections for the beloved, so the soul seeks nothing else but the presence and the will of the Beloved.

This is the consummation stage of our baptismal consecration to Jesus, or, if you prefer, our Marian consecration. For Mary was totally docile to the slightest inspirations of the Holy Spirit. The Spirit possessed her as spouse at the annunciation, sped her to her cousin in need, gave her a heart that pondered the mysteries of God's action in her life, directed her in the obscurity of Nazareth as she formed Jesus in his childhood, supported her at the cross, and used her as model of response to his outpouring on Pentecost.

That is why Mary is our great teacher of docility to the Holy Spirit. The Holy Spirit did not become incarnate as did the Word, the Second Person of the Holy Trinity. He has no face of his own, so to speak. Yet he often assumes the face of Mary as a means of interpreting his movement for us in loving, human, maternal terms. This happens in authentic Marian apparitions. It also happens daily in the lives of the saints who are closely united to Mary.

Here we are in the realm of the mystical union of love to which every Christian is called but to which few actually attain. Sexual imagery for this union is used extensively in the Song of Songs, especially as interpreted in the church's rich mystical tradition. Sexual temptations often derive their strength from a vacuum in personal relationships. The hunger on which they feed is a hunger for personal union and intimacy. Perhaps that is the reason Scripture uses sexual language to express God's call to each of us and to the entire church to be intimately joined to him. Sexual temptations can even remind us of that call to intimacy!

THE CHURCH WITHOUT SPOT OR WRINKLE

As one matures in this relationship of docility to the Spirit, one becomes aware that there is also a corporate dimension to it. We desire that the church be the Lord's perfect bride, so we love the whole church and desire that she be united in love so as to be more worthy of her spouse. We no longer lapse into childish "put downs" of other communities or parishes or schools, comparing them unfavorably with our own. In a report one of Fr. Chaminade's disciples prepared for the civil officials in France, there was a comparison of the Marianists unfavorable to the Jesuits. In response Fr. Chaminade said he admired the work they have done. "But if I permit myself to be compared with them, I would lie regarding the past, and I would promise more than I can regarding the future. All that, my dear Son, is only a lot of words which might be called ambitious for merit, vanity of vanities, temptations we must strip ourselves of and especially defend ourselves against."[2]

It is a great temptation, in countries where the church is well established, to become competitive even within the church, to become religiously chauvinist, to carve out little kingdoms and jealously protect them against possible encroachments, even by other church groups. When I returned to the United States after six years in the missions in South Asia, I was shocked at the extent to which the church here had become polarized. It seemed to be feeding on its own internal problems rather than being zealous for its mission to evangelize. Liberals and conservatives were firing volleys at one another, and the real enemy seemed to be chortling with delight. In Catholic institutions, I often found people shooting spiritual spitwads at each other, while the whole institution was under attack by the big guns of secularism.

In missionary territories, where survival is often the most one can hope for, I have often found it easier to feel mutual support and interdependence among the laborers in the harvest. In any case, to be a spouse of Christ is to long not only for union with him but for unity in his church. For we become more and more one with that church which is the spouse of Christ, the spouse he wishes to come before him without spot or wrinkle (Eph 5:27).

This does not mean that we condemn the church as such, for Jesus reminds us that in this world there will be weeds among the wheat in the field and garfish as well as trout in the net. He tells us that we should be as patient with the fig tree as the Father is, doing what we can to nurture it back to life. But we do suffer with its blights and we long to see it more beautiful. St. Catherine of Siena is one of the outstanding models of this love for the church. She was a great contemplative, but precisely because she was so caught up in the intimate life of the Trinity, she felt passionately about the sad state of the church in her day, and even counseled the pope.

It is just such docility to the Holy Spirit, in this consummation stage of discipleship, that enables God to inspire in his loved ones great works for the kingdom. Mother Teresa was on a narrow-gauge train climbing the hills up to Siliguri, in eastern India, when the Holy Spirit inspired her to found the Missionaries of Charity. Fr. Chaminade received a similar inspiration after spending long hours at the foot of a shrine to Our Lady of the Pillar in Zaragoza, Spain. On his return to Bordeaux from exile in 1800, he became such an effective instrument that the bishop later said that every good work in those first decades in his diocese could be traced to Fr. Chaminade. And the ultimate fruit was the founding of several lay and religious communities.

Not all of us, of course, are called to found religious communities. We are called, however, to become so transformed by the Holy Spirit that he can use us for whatever he chooses to bring God's kingdom on earth.

Meditations

Jesus tells us we cannot follow self and be guided by him at the same time (Lk 9:23-24). Only the pure of heart will see God (Mt 5:8). Our God is a consuming fire (Heb 12:29). The victor is clothed in white and belongs totally to the Lord (Rv 3:5). The spouse of the Lamb is without spot or wrinkle (Eph 5:27). Be led by the Spirit and you will not do the deeds of the flesh (Rom 8:1-17).

Exercises

• There are two words in this chapter which our modern culture does not value. They are: detachment and self-denial. Reflect on what these two words mean to you. What are some areas in your life where you may have an inappropriate attachment to individuals, things, certain behaviors, or certain attitudes? Do your attachments stand in the way of your spiritual maturity? What are some of the things you can begin to do to respond to God's call to detach yourself from whatever blocks your progress to him?

- In prayer, ask Mary to show you some good things in your life that will be enhanced by your practice of this virtue.

Steps on the Journey

1. How would your day look if you were totally docile to the movements of the Holy Spirit? How can Mary be a model for you of this docility? What do you need to do to be more aware of the gentle invitations of the Holy Spirit? Remember the Holy Spirit is identified with God's love (Rom 5:5).

2. Do you really love the church, not just your local community or parish, but your diocese, the church in your country, the universal church? Do you avoid putting down other parts of the body of Christ? Where you perceive the body is weak, do you intercede instead of gossip or condemn?

Heavenly Father, I am so inwardly insecure at times that I cling to persons, things, positions, and my reputation. Keep my eyes so focused on your infinite love and mercy toward me that I may be able to let go of these things and, like a trusting child, run toward you with arms that are free and open. With Mary as my guide and inspiration, show me how I may let the Holy Spirit take over my life and make me available for the dreams you have for your church and your world. Amen.

TWENTY-FOUR

Freedom from and for the World

❧

The "world" is an ambiguous concept. Perhaps the most famous verse in Scripture tells us, "God so loved the world that he gave his only Son" (Jn 3:16). This is the same world which the Second Vatican Council instructed us to embrace, with all its hopes and fears, all its joys and sufferings (see *The Pastoral Constitution on The Church in the Modern World, Gaudium et spes*).

Yet John also writes, "Do not love the world or the things that are in the world. If anyone loves the world, the love of the Father is not in him" (1 Jn 2:15). He continues on in the next verse to explain the negative sense of this same word: "All that is in the world is the lure of the flesh, the lure of the eyes, and pride in one's possessions" (v. 16).

FREEDOM FROM THE WORLD

According to Scripture, the "world" to be renounced is not the physical creation pronounced good by God, nor the human beings he commanded to rule over it. Rather John refers to false values, those which suggest that this world is the only world, and that we should squeeze out of it every drop of pleasure, selfish or otherwise. In particular, the "world" in this sense means cupidity, greed, the spirit of possessiveness.

Religious make a vow of poverty as a means of shedding this worldly spirit. But doing so offers no guarantee that the spirit of possessiveness is dead. By the same token, laity who retain personal ownership of their goods are not thereby condemned to a life consumed by greed. They too are called to inner freedom regarding the world and its values. Jesus made no exception when he said, "Whoever does not renounce all he possesses cannot be my disciple" (Lk 14:33).

We discussed this kind of detachment in the last chapter in relation to our spousal union with the Lord and docility to the Holy Spirit. Here we look at the same mystery in relation to the world in which we live, that world for which we pray when we say, "Thy kingdom come." To be free to embrace the world as God does, we must first be free of the grip the world has on us.

This spirit of detachment from the world and its values touches more than material goods. It covers any attachment we might have to job, place, person, time, secrets, wardrobe—anything that would hinder us from being able to say, "God alone." Having met this challenge in various ways in the virtues of preparation and in the work of purification, we are now concerned with the consummation of this virtue. This freedom to which we are called here reveals in yet another way the human face of faith, hope, and love. One who reaches this stage will experience remarkable freedom in regard to everything that is not God.

Let me share a personal example. One day I wrote in my journal:

I have come to realize (with John of the Cross and others) that there is an emptiness in my heart that I constantly seek to fill—either with little "needs," or with activity. This passion to fill betrays the fact that I do not want to face and accept my radical emptiness as a creature—as one who is nothing but *capacity* for the infinite. The passion to keep filling more and more is simply a testimony that "You have made our hearts for you, and they are restless until they rest in you."

The psalmist said it long before Augustine: "In God alone is my soul at rest" (Ps 62:1). And Jesus said that in him we would find rest for our souls. Often, when I begin to pray—that is, when I enter that space of God which is supposed to be empty of other things—I find my heart and mind rushing immediately to some "filler"—a need unmet or an activity undone. This simply shows how much my ego fears to be empty. But empty it must be if you, Lord, are to fill it—for that is what you want to do.

May I have the heart of Mary, empty of all and filled with the All which is you.

FREEDOM FOR THE WORLD

Persons progressing in this inner liberty will be especially effective in the apostolate, for it will be obvious to others that they are not self-serving in any way, that they are willing to give anything away if charity demands it. They will also find joy in working with the poor and disadvantaged.

Not everyone who champions the poor and disadvantaged, of course, has necessarily been perfected in this virtue. A young man I knew spoke out for the poor and condemned the rich at every opportunity he got, but he told me years later (now married and a stockbroker) that much of it was anger at his own father. Healed of that anger and now having to raise a family, he had come to realize that there are generous "gospel poor" even among the rich. One of my seminarians has now as a priest spent most of his active years living among the poor and working for their development in India and Bangladesh. He has been a close friend and occa-

sional retreat director for Mother Teresa and her sisters,
since he is a kindred spirit with them in his love for the poor.
I can't say whether he has reached perfection in living this
virtue. All I know is that he has a tremendous heart for the
poor. Rather than getting angry at the rich, he has brought
many of them on board by giving them the opportunity to
respond to the gospel by helping the poor.

Those who have received the grace of poverty of spirit feel
so enriched by God that they want to give of their riches
without expecting any return. Like Jesus, they have become
poor for the sake of others, that others might become rich
(2 Cor 8:9). They become available for the great works of
God.

Instead of being possessed by the world, those who reach
this level of freedom possess the world by joyously serving it
as Jesus did. At the beginning of Jesus' ministry, the devil
offered him the whole world—at the price of idolatry. The
Son rejected that path and instead followed his Father's will
to the cross. By dying for the world being held in the grip of
Satan, Jesus won what he had refused to gain by idolatry.
The world was now his: "All authority in heaven and on
earth has been given to me" (Mt 28:18). In that mysterious
"owning" of the world and all it holds we too share because
of our belonging to Jesus: "All are yours... the world, life,
death, the present, the future—all are yours, and you are
Christ's, and Christ is God's" (1 Cor 3:21-23).

Consequently, being totally conformed to Jesus and Mary
means that we do not run away from the world. Rather we
are plunged into it as servants to bring the world God's
redeeming and transforming love. In doing so we also experience freedom from its idolatrous grip.

Is this a distant summit to which most of us can only
aspire? Perhaps. But that's where God is calling us. We need
to take the step he asks of us today. Mary will show us how.
She is the leader, both in her life and in her song, of those
poor whom the Lord lifts up (Lk 1:52). Like her, they know

that they are merely the lowly servants of the Lord (Lk 1:38, 48). Because all they have has been freely given them, they, like her, can freely give (Lk 10:8). To love and belong to Mary is to love and belong to the poor. Perhaps that is why she appears by preference to the young and the poor.

Meditations

Jesus teaches us to renounce all (Lk 14:33). God's love dispels worldly love (1 Jn 2:15). When we seek his kingdom, everything else is given to us (Mt 6:33; 1 Cor 3:22-23). Blessed are the poor in spirit (Mt 5:3). Leaving all, we become fishers of people (Mt 4:19). See other references in the chapter above.

Steps on the Journey

1. What does being "free" and "available" to God mean in your life?

2. Whatever your vocation may be, you will find there your first responsibility to God. What does this mean for you as a single person, married person, parent, professed religious, or priest? What are some practical ways in your occupation in which you can become totally open to God?

3. Sometimes the desire to "flee the world" can be simply a resistance to God's call to love and serve the people he has placed in our lives. Jesus, after all, ministered to outcasts and sinners. When we are truly possessed by the love of God, we will feel the urge to reach out to the abandoned and the marginalized. Is there an element of this outreach in your life? Can your prayer life be authentic without it?

4. When you contemplate Mary, do you see her eyes reflecting the needs of the poor? How do you respond?

Lord Jesus, I have come to realize that "the world" is not "out there" somewhere, but something of which I am a part. I am part of this good and beautiful world you have made, but I'm also part of the sinful world that turns away from you. Let the world that is in me become your kingdom. Make my heart a pure vessel for the Father's love, like Mary's. Then I will be able to touch the world with your redeeming power. Amen.

Afterword

No book can say everything. But every good book on growing in the Christian life should point us to our final end in Christ. After all, the ultimate good of our lives is not our own holiness or virtue but the enjoyment of God himself. It is called the *beatific* vision because it is the face-to-face vision of God of which all human longings are only foreshadowings. It is light that is also fire, the consuming fire of God's infinite love in which we are so immersed that we seem to "become God," like the iron that seems to become the very fire into which it is plunged.

In this fire, which is the Holy Spirit, we know the Father and the Son. We are caught up in their mutual embrace which no word can describe, no image contain, no song express. For only the Spirit of God knows God fully (1 Cor 2:11). That Spirit is ours even now, but it is only a foretaste of what we shall become (Rom 5:5; 1 Jn 3:2-3).

Mary already enjoys that vision. She is already transformed even bodily by that fire. If she, Lady Wisdom, invites us to follow the lowly path that she and her Son walked on earth, it is only that our hearts may be more and more capable of the joy that is hers. For to her Jesus has already said what one day, please God, he will say to us: "Enter into the joy of your Lord!" (Mt 25:23).

May the Father, the Son, and the Holy Spirit be glorified in all places through the Immaculate Virgin Mary! Amen.

Notes

ONE
Images of Spiritual Growth

1. One can get a further idea of the richness and variety of images for the growth of the Christian life from David A. Fleming, S.M., *The Fire and the Cloud* (New York: Paulist, 1978).

2. See F. Kelly Nemeck and M. Theresa Coombs, *The Spiritual Journey* (Collegeville, Minn.: Liturgical Press, 1991), especially 228-31.

THREE
Becoming a New Creation

1. "Tongues" is a real stumbling block for some people. Although mentioned as a gift of the Spirit, speaking in tongues even in Paul's day was not expected of everyone (1 Cor 12:30). Our verbally oriented culture can make it more difficult to appreciate this way of praying. But it is mentioned as late as the time of St. Augustine in what he called *jubilation*: "Words cannot express the things that are sung by the heart. Take the case of people singing while harvesting in the fields or in the vineyards or when any other strenuous work is in progress. Although they begin by giving expression to their happiness in sung words, yet shortly there is a change. As if so happy that words can no longer express what they feel, they discard the restricting syllables. They burst into a simple sound of joy, of jubilation. Such a cry of joy is a sound signifying that the heart is bringing to birth what it cannot utter in words. Now, who is more worthy of such a cry of jubilation than God himself, whom all words fail to describe? If words will not serve, and yet you must not remain silent, what else can you do but cry out for joy? Your heart must rejoice beyond words, soaring into an immensity of gladness, unrestrained by syllabic bonds." (*In Ps 32*, sermon, 7-8; *Corpus Christianorum Latinorum 38*, 253-254. Used in the Breviary of the Feast of St. Cecilia, November 22).

2. Even into the fourth century we find St. Hilary saying: "We who have been reborn through the sacrament of baptism experience intense joy when we feel within us the first stirrings of the Holy Spirit. We begin to have insight into the mysteries of faith, we are able to prophesy and to speak with wisdom. We become steadfast in hope and receive the gifts of healing." (*In Ps* 64:15; *Corpus Scriptorum Ecclesticorum Latinorum* 22:246).

FOUR
The Gift of Mary

1. *True Devotion to the Blessed Virgin* (Bay Shore, NY: Montfort Publications, 1987), No. 120.
2. What follows is a summary of a much more extensive development in my book, *Our Father, Our Mother: Mary and the Faces of God* (Steubenville, OH: Franciscan University Press, 1990), 71-143.
3. See Montague, *Our Father, Our Mother*, 116-28.
4. If one wishes to use this prayer for community recitation, the singular "I," "my," and "mine" may readily be converted to the plural "we" forms.

FIVE
Faith of the Heart

1. *Spirit of Our Foundation* (Dayton, Ohio: St. Mary's Convent, 1911) I, No. 224.
2. For an excellent treatment of God's providence in our lives see F. Kelly Nemeck and M. Theresa Coombs, *The Spiritual Journey*, 21-32.
3. *Spirit of Our Foundation* I, No. 213.
4. *Spirit of Our Foundation* I, No. 219.
5. *Spirit of Our Foundation* I, No. 229.

SIX
Bringing Our Bodies to Jesus

1. For a full explanation of this exercise see Anthony de Mello, *Sadhana* (New York: Doubleday, 1978), 9-11.
2. If food is your compulsion, try meditating on Sirach 37:26-30: "My son, while you are well, govern your appetite/ so that you allow it not what is bad for you;/ for not every food is good for everyone,/ nor is everything suited to every taste./ Be not drawn after every enjoyment,/ neither become a glutton for choice foods,/ for sickness comes with overeating,/ and gluttony brings on biliousness./ Through lack of self-control many have died,/ but the abstemious man prolongs his life" (NAB).
3. Further exercises may be found in de Mello, *Sadhana*, exercises 2, 3, 8, 9, 10.

ELEVEN

Order in the Control Room: Transforming The Present

1. Ten typical mental distortions are listed by David Burns, M.D., in his book, *Feeling Good: The New Mood Therapy* (New York: Signet, 1980), 40-41. I highly recommend this book and its companion volume, *The Feeling Good Handbook* (New York: Penguin, 1989). They contain practical exercises for correcting your way of thinking and thus exerting better control over your feelings.

FOURTEEN

Interdependent Cooperators

1. Pope John Paul II, *Encyclical: On the Dignity and Vocation of Women* (Boston: Daughters of St. Paul, 1988), No. 24. Pope John Paul II in his encyclical *On the Dignity of Woman* explains the passage in Ephesians 5:21-30 thus: The teaching about the headship of the husband and the obedience of the wife is drawn from the culture of the times. It still has its validity, but the author of Ephesians brings to it a specifically Christian principle in the light of which it is to be applied: *mutual submission*. That is, both husband and wife are to submit to each other in love, respecting the particular gifts with which each is endowed.

TWENTY-ONE

All Is Gift

1. William Joseph Chaminade, *Marianist Direction I* (Dayton: Marianist Publications, 1966) No. 610.

2. Jacques Olier, *Introduction à la vie et aux vertus chrétiennes* (Paris: Migne, 1856), col. 82.

TWENTY-TWO

Living Only for God's Glory

1. William Joseph Chaminade, *Marianist Direction III* (Dayton, Ohio: Marianist Publications, 1969), 33.

TWENTY-THREE

The Cross and the Spirit

1. William Joseph Chaminade quoting Jacques Olier, *Marianist Direction III* (Dayton, Ohio: Marianist Publications, 1969), 461.

2. *Lettres de M. Chaminade* (Nivelles: Havaux, 1930) II, No. 383, p. 152. My translation. Alternate translation of Chaminade's letters available (Marianist Resources Commission, Dayton, Ohio, 1976).

Other Books on Mary of Special
Interest to Servant Readers

Praying the Scriptural Rosary
Msgr. David E. Rosage

Now you can pray the scriptural rosary with greater understanding by using the invaluable helps in this attractive prayer book. The text includes a Scripture verse, short meditation, and prayer response keyed to each Hail Mary in every mystery of the rosary. For each mystery an entire set of verses, meditations, and responses are taken primarily from the New Testament—a corresponding set focuses on Old Testament passages. *$6.99*

A Marian Prayer Book
A Treasury of Prayers, Hymns, and Meditations
Edited by Pam Moran

Whether you already have a devotion to Mary or are interested in getting to know her better, here are heartfelt prayers, meditations, and hymns that not only develop key Marian themes, but help you form a deeper prayer relationship with her. A Marian Prayer Book is an ideal gift book for loved ones and an important prayer resource for your family and parish. *$7.99*

Available at your Christian bookstore or from:

Servant Publications ✳ Dept. 209 ✳ P.O. Box 7455
Ann Arbor, Michigan 48107
Please include payment plus $2.75 per book
for postage and handling.
*Send for our FREE catalog of Christian
books, music, and cassettes.*